The Sir Winston Method

The

SIR WINSTON
METHOD

··········

The Five Secrets of Speaking the Language of Leadership

James C. Humes

William Morrow and Company, Inc.

New York

It is the policy of William Morrow and Company, Inc., and its imprints and affiliates, recognizing the importance of preserving what has been written, to print the books we publish on acid-free paper, and we exert our best efforts to that end.

Library of Congress Cataloging-in-Publication Data

Humes, James C.
The Sir Winston method : the five secrets of speaking the language
of leadership / James C. Humes.
p.   cm.
Includes index.
ISBN 0-688-10224-7
1. Public speaking.   2. Churchill, Winston, Sir, 1874–1965—
Oratory.   I. Title.
PN4121.H858   1991
808.5'1—dc20   90-26201
                                                              CIP

Printed in the United States of America

First Edition

1 2 3 4 5 6 7 8 9 10

BOOK DESIGN BY RICHARD ORIOLO

To Rufus,
Whose steadfast loyalty and
dedication recall that of another
Rufus to Sir Winston himself

Acknowledgments

...

I thank Bill Adler for giving me the idea of such a book and Maria Guarnaschelli for her superb editing and tailoring of my manuscript.

I am always indebted to J. D. Williams and his law firm, particularly Lourdes Z. Monson.

I also want to mention my old friends, Don Whitehead, Jim Ring, Trevor Armbrister, Bill Schulz, and Jim Spardy at the Fels Institute of the University of Pennsylvania for giving me the opportunity to teach at the graduate level.

C o n t e n t s

...

1. Not for Presidents Only   *11*

2. Fear Is a Friend   *15*

3. Churchill: "There Is in That Act of Preparing the Moment You Start Caring"   *23*

4. The Ear Is One-tenth the Organ of the Eye   *27*

5. Sir Winston's Formula   *31*

6. Sir Winston's Rule Number One: *Strong Beginning*   *33*

7. Sir Winston's Rule Number Two: *One Theme*   *43*

8. Sir Winston's Rule Number Three: *Simple Language*   *51*

9. Sir Winston's Rule Number Four: *Pictures*   *61*

10

...

CONTENTS

10. Sir Winston's Rule Number Five:
    Emotional Ending   73

    11. The Speech-a-matic   *81*

    12. The Magic Quote Maker   *87*

    13. Quote Like a Leader   *103*

    14. Conference Charisma   *111*

    15. Boffo Intros   *117*

    16. Going for the Green   *123*

    17. A Prop, Not a Crutch   *129*

    18. At Wits' End   *135*

    19. The King and You   *147*

    20. Read a Speech Like Reagan   *157*

    21. Talk Your Way to the Top   *171*

    Index   *179*

O n e

NOT FOR
PRESIDENTS
ONLY

· · · · · · · · · ·

Speaking Is Not
Just a Speech to the
Rotary Club

Why do you need another "speech" book? You say the last time you spoke it was to the Rotary Club when you headed the heart drive. And now your spouse has made you swear off leading any more drives until you clean out the garage or give up golf. That means never!

The answer is that this is not a speech

book; it's a leadership book! If it's a how-to book, it's how to motivate, how to inspire, in other words, *how to lead*. Answer these questions honestly:

1. In your pep talk to the last sales meeting, did you sound more like a Joe Schmoe than a Joe Paterno?

2. Did your presentation at the last planning session fizzle flat?

3. When you hand out awards at a company luncheon, do you repeat the same trite dribble everyone else does?

4. When you have to introduce someone, do you just read out a résumé?

5. Finally, if you are asked to say a few words or more, do you regard it as a *chore* and not as a *chance* to grab the brass ring?

Those who rise to the top know more than just the bottom line. My Democratic friends say Ronald Reagan knew less about foreign policy after eight years as President than Richard Nixon did before he entered the White House. Certainly he knew less about Congress than Senators Bob Dole or Howard Baker, his Republican rivals in 1980, and surely, he had less experience than another rival, George Bush, who in 1980 had already served as UN ambassador, liaison to China, and head of the CIA.

Yet the American Academy of Political Scientists (which cannot be called a right-wing group) called the Reagan presidency the most successful in getting its ideals carried out since Franklin D. Roosevelt, another master communicator.

Reagan may not have been a hands-on administrator, but when the "Great Communicator" spoke, people did not sit on their hands. He motivated; he inspired; he led. What was his secret?

Well, like Franklin Roosevelt and Winston Churchill, he knew the *language of leadership.*

What if you don't aim to be President of the United States? Do you think about becoming the chief executive of the company you're now with or maybe sometime heading up your own business?

Do you think Lee Iacocca would have become head of Chrysler if he hadn't known the language of leadership? If Winston Churchill saved his country by his speeches, so did Iacocca save Chrysler by his words.

Back in the 1960's a thirtyish executive in Philadelphia became head of the biggest bank in Pennsylvania. How did he pull that off? Through his superior management and business skills? No, he did it by his ability to talk to groups both inside the bank and outside. The fact that the bank operation later collapsed in the seventies only reinforces my point. Others who knew more about banking were passed over for the top job. It's not enough to have better skills and more experience—unless you can communicate that experience and skills. He (or she) who looks and talks like a leader gets leadership positions.

Every time you have to speak—whether it's in an auditorium, in a company conference room, or even at your own desk—you are auditioning for leadership.

The difference between mere management and leadership is communication. And that art of communication is the *language of leadership*.

T w o

FEAR IS A
FRIEND

· · · · · · · · · ·

Greatest Speaker in History
Fainted out of Fear in
One of His First Speeches

What if you were interviewing a job applicant and the young man before you not
only stuttered but had a lisp? When you
looked at his résumé, you learned that he
had no college degree, in fact never attended college. Then you heard from a
colleague that the applicant had fainted
out of fear in one of his first public presentations.

Well, if you had rejected him, you would have dismissed Winston Churchill.

Fear Is a Friend

If your knees shake a bit when you get up to talk, join the club—the biggest club in the world.

Some years ago a pollster reported in the *Reader's Digest* the three greatest fears. Number three was dying, number two was cancer, but the first was speaking in front of an audience.

A friend of mine had the opportunity to watch Mario Cuomo up close from the side as the New York governor delivered his masterful keynote address at the Democratic National Convention in San Francisco in 1984. He reported that he could see Cuomo's knees shake like an old washing machine as he listened to his introduction and that they didn't stop knocking until he was well into his speech. And Cuomo is one of the greatest orators in America today.

Helen Hayes, the First Lady of American Theater, with more than sixty years as a performer onstage, admitted that she still got butterflies at eighty!

After six decades she was still nervous. But the jitters before the curtain rose was not a foe but a friend—"a familiar companion that nagged me to do my very best.

"Don't think of a fear as a deterrent," she said. "It's a kick in the rear to prepare."

In other words, don't let it intimidate you; let it be an

incentive, an incentive to practice and prepare. Fear shouldn't be a constraint but your conscience telling your mind and body to get in gear.

Fear Is Energy

What is fear, after all, but emotional energy? Turn those nerves into nervous energy—that psychological edge—that can turn the would-be drone into a dynamo.

Let's put that fear under the microscope. It's fear of looking foolish. Do you know what psychologists say is the most familiar nightmare experienced before a talk? The sleeper imagines he is caught in a situation where he is the only one without any clothes.

By the way, Churchill, as a psychological antidote, used to look out at his audience and imagine they all were naked. Actually Churchill worked out a more practical formula to master fear.

Mask Your Mannerisms

Churchill found part of his solution in overcoming fear in recalling his military days patrolling the Afghan border in northern India. As an officer he couldn't let his men see that he was scared. "But only a fool," said Churchill, "is not afraid of being shot at."

So Churchill masked those mannerisms that suggested

fear. He stopped gripping the lectern as if it were a raft in some ocean-swirling tide.

He stopped racing through his speech as if he were running through a gauntlet of swords on a pirate ship. He made himself speak deliberately—in measured sentences.

Finally, he stopped staring fixedly down at the lectern as if the audience were full of monstrous Medusas, a look at whose faces could turn you into stone. He forced himself to look out at his audience and engage their eyes.

Don't Make Excuses

Then he adopted the British Foreign Office motto: "Never excuse, never explain, never complain." When a speaker opens by alibiing, "I'm not a very good speaker" or "I didn't have much time to prepare," he is not taking out an insurance policy in case he flops; he is only planting in his audience's mind the likelihood of his failure.

If they don't know, don't give them a hint.

Churchill once proposed marriage to the actress Ethel Barrymore (she turned him down, saying there wasn't room on center stage for both of them). Barrymore, who came from an acting family and began her stage career at three, told him she never quite overcame her jitters, but "Winston," she said, "you've got to put on an act!"

So when you have to stand up and talk, put on an act—and cover up those telltale gestures that suggest you're quaking in your boots.

Churchill's next step in fighting feelings of fear is the key one.

Master the Material

When Churchill collapsed while speaking early in his House of Commons career, it wasn't his first speech. In his maiden address, he had spoken of his recent experiences in the Boer War, and he did fairly well.

But in his second speech he attempted too much. He attacked the prime minister on a wide range of issues—taxes, education, foreign policy. And that is when he collapsed in the middle of his talk.

Churchill failed because he bit off more than he could chew. No one—not even a Churchill—can master the subjects of finance, foreign policy, and education for a single speech.

Why did he try? Like a lot of us, he didn't think he would have enough to say, so he picked too many topics to talk about.

Don't Bite Off
More Than You Can Chew

When my daughter Mary was in the seventh grade, she said, "Daddy, I have a hundred-word history report I have to write for my social studies class, and I've chosen World War Two."

"All of World War Two!" I replied. "Why not write about one battle or, better yet, one day of one battle? You want to know why: The teacher won't know anything about it!"

A lady came back to me from China in 1976 and said, "Mr. Humes, I want your help on a speech."

I answered, "What's your topic?"

She said, "China." My dumbfounded look was my answer, so she amended and added, "Post-Mao China."

"You're a schoolteacher," I told her. "Why not write about education in China or, better yet, the first grade in China?"

In other words, whittle down your subject to a manageable size.

By the way, my daughter later won honors in classics at Harvard. When I congratulated her, she said "Daddy, I owe it all to you. My honors paper was 'The Evolution of Anklewear as It Appears on Grecian Urns in the Hellenistic Era.'" That's really knowing a lot about very little!

Try to speak on what you know about, and if you don't have firsthand experience, narrow your subject matter down to something you can easily master.

When you have butterflies, it's because you're afraid of looking stupid. But if you give the audience information on something it doesn't know about—in a simple, easy-to-take-away form—you've done all that was expected of you.

FEAR IS A FRIEND

Know More About Your Subject Than Anyone in the Audience

Focus your subject. Don't talk about loans; talk about loans financed by the equity in a house. Don't talk about the stock market; talk about pharmaceutical stocks.

When I took my bar exam cram course, the instructor said, "Look, guys, on the day of examination you'll know more law than anyone else. You may forget it the next week, but for one day you're an expert."

When you narrow your subject, you're making sure that you know more about it than anyone else in the audience. How can you be scared when you know more about the subject than anyone else on that particular day?

CHURCHILL: "THERE IS IN THAT ACT OF PREPARING THE MOMENT YOU START CARING"

....

Do you remember back in college or high school when you were assigned a report to write? First it was a chore that you put off doing. But when you finally got down to it, what at first seemed boring became interesting. The more you read, the more you got involved. The more committed you got, the more you cared about what you wrote. Churchill described it: "There is in that act of preparing the moment you start caring."

Only then are you ready to speak to an audience. Because an audience can be *convinced* only when they see you *care* about what you are talking about.

Churchill had a father figure who taught him about speaking. He was an Irish-born American politician named Bourke Cockran. Probably you've never heard of him, although Presidents Wilson and Taft said he was America's greatest orator. He was the only one ever to keynote three national conventions. Incidentally, Cockran, who was a onetime lover of Churchill's mother, also coached Franklin Roosevelt. Churchill once asked Cockran, "Bourke, what is the secret of eloquence?" and he replied: "Believing in what you are talking about." Cockran summed it up in one word: "sincerity."

It doesn't matter how many statistics or facts you rattle off—if the audience senses that you aren't really committed.

A writer friend of mine in Washington woke up one morning to find his left arm paralyzed. He couldn't feel a thing in his left hand. He rushed to the office of a neurosurgeon in Bethesda who administered to Presidents as well as Navy brass in a nearby hospital.

He told the doctor about his arm. The doctor in a heavy German accent replied, "Do not fear. You haf come to the right place. See that certificate on the wall. I vas graduated from the University of Vienna."

My friend said, "Doctor, my hand, I can't feel a thing!"

"... THE MOMENT YOU START CARING"

"It is nothing. I am expert in the field. See that other certificate. I vas elected to the Royal Academy of Neurosurgeons."

"But, Doctor, did I have a stroke? I can't feel—"

"Be patient. You are in goot hands. See that other certificate. That's for ven I addressed the Vorld Institute of—"

With that, my friend left and went to his neighborhood doctor, who told him, "Trevor, you just slept on your arm. If the feeling doesn't come back by dinnertime, give me a call."

The word is this: *People don't care how much you know unless they know how much you care!*

THE EAR IS
ONE-TENTH
THE ORGAN OF
THE EYE

· · · · · · · · · ·

In March 1983 I was in Newport, Rhode Island, to deliver an afternoon seminar. When I walked into the hotel coffee shop to have breakfast, I heard my name being called out: "James Humes, isn't it? Will you join me?"

I looked up and saw a man whose face I knew but whose name couldn't place.

But the politician in me—I served in the Pennsylvania legislature in my twenties—made me try to make up in warmth and affection what I lacked in memory. "Hey, how the hell are you? Why, you look more distinguished than ever!" Actually he did look quite elegant in his tweedy jacket and polka-dot ascot. Then breakfast was ordered and eaten, but I still couldn't remember his name though he told me we'd met in London when I was writing my Churchill biography.

By the third cup of coffee I had ransacked my brain for the name of my breakfast companion, tossing out every conversational gambit except the traditional, one which I saved to the very end: "Tell me, how's the family?" His stricken face flashed his name as soon as I had blurted out my line. It was Claus von Bulow, the aristocratic socialite accused of attempting to murder his wife in Newport. The criminal court action had been brought by his stepchildren.

It was like saying, "Mrs. Lincoln, did you enjoy the play last night?"

The fact is that we have in the mind bank—that is, memory—thousands of faces but not the names that go with them.

The ear is one-tenth the organ of the eye.

Speakers suffer from the delusion that every word they utter reaches the listener's ear. Wrong! There is no tube that carries all your words to the listener's ear. When you read, every word may reach your eye, but when you listen, not every word registers in the ear.

In visual terms it is as if the audience saw you through

a gauzy screen. That is why a talk should have more the bold lines of a cartoon caricature drawing than the detail of a photograph.

Think back to school days. Remember when the instructor marked in the margin of your report "redundant" when you were repetitious. Well, if being repetitious is a *vice* in an article, it is a *device* in a speech.

Compare an article with a speech this way. An article is like an ordinary lamp, but a speech is like the tensor light you use when you want to read in bed while your mate sleeps. A tensor light covers a much smaller area than a lamp, but it does it more brightly, more *intensively*. In a talk you can't convey all the facts or statistics you would in an article. But those that you do use have to be focused for impact.

A Speech or Talk Is Not an Article or Report to Be Read Aloud

A speech or talk should be *the oral projection of your personality, experiences, and ideas*.

F i v e

SIR WINSTON'S
FORMULA

....

The Churchill Notes

When Winston Churchill was a young lieutenant patrolling Queen Victoria's empire in such far-flung outposts as the Afghan Himalayas or the Sudan Sahara, he spent his spare time in his tent reading the great speeches—speeches by William Pitt, Benjamin Disraeli, and our own Abraham Lincoln. Then, when he was

THE SIR WINSTON METHOD

back in London on leave, he'd go to the House of Commons and listen to the top speakers.

At the age of twenty-three he jotted down his observations. The key lesson he learned was that a speech was not an article; *it must be geared to the ear*. He wrote these notes for himself—not to be published. I learned of these notes from his family, and I call them the language of leadership.

SIR WINSTON'S
RULE NUMBER
ONE: STRONG
BEGINNING

....

Prime Time

Do you know when you have the greatest attention of the audience? Right after the introduction. The audience is waiting to see what you look like, what you sound like.

Yet too many speakers waste that psychological advantage with meaningless small talk. Churchill said, *"Opening amenities are often opening inanities."*

It's *Not* a Pleasure . . .

Churchill refused even to begin by saying, "It's an honor to speak to the . . ." He once told an associate, "I never say, 'It gives me great pleasure,' to speak to any audience because there are only a few activities from which I derive intense pleasure and speaking is not one of them."

To Churchill, it was like saying, "How are you?" Audiences won't remember at the end of your conversation whether you said it or not.

If you really want to say something nice about the organization or if you have to single out a few in the audience for special mention, save it for the middle of the speech, when it is believed.

Churchill believed that *praise in the beginning of the speech comes off as flattery; the same praise in the middle of the speech comes off as sincerity.*

Power of the Parenthetical Praise

Some years ago I told this at a seminar for the cadets at the Virginia Military Institute in Lexington, Virginia: "If you say to the young lady just as she gets in the car, 'You look nice,' you get no points; it's expected. But if you say at the candlelit dinner in the restaurant, 'My, that brooch really brings out the beautiful blue of your eyes,' that's points!"

RULE NUMBER ONE: STRONG BEGINNING

When you've finished preparing your remarks, look for a paragraph that suggests a *parenthesis*.

("And speaking of teamwork, no one exemplifies this more than this Rotary Club in the cleanup drive it organized last month.")

("By the way, when you talk about leadership, we all were inspired by Mayor Jenkins's resolute action in pushing for a new sewage plant.")

I guarantee you that every time you single out one or two for a parenthetical praise, they'll be the first after the talk to tell you what a fine speech you gave!

Last year I gave my "Language of Leadership" talk to Republican senators at a West Virginia weekend conference. Later three senators phoned me to say the best advice I gave them was to begin with a powerful statement and do away with the opening amenities.

Do you know the format of most of the talks given by top executives? They begin with "It's an honor . . ." Then they segue into "And it's great to see John. I remember golfing with him last year at Burning Tree Club, my slice was worse than his putts."* They follow that up with "That reminds me of a story." And they go on to retell some joke heard at the Rotary Club or country club bar. Oh, they may get polite laughter, but that's more out of respect to the speakers than reaction to their joke. Then after the joke they pull out a redraft of a trade association article and read it.

---

* If you want to mention someone's golf or tennis game, try the parenthetical praise: "By the way, the reports you read recently about a falling market are as far off as my slice. Your John Rodgers can tell you about that. I played with him at Burning Tree last week."

Do you think that format qualifies as a speech? It's the shell of a speech—a charade.

Old Jokes, Like
Old Pistols, Can Backfire

Some executives think there is an Eleventh Commandment: "Thou shalt begin every speech with a joke." Why does the prestigious speaker whose picture adorns *Fortune* magazine or the scientist who was honored in Stockholm with a Nobel Prize think he has to be one of the boys and begin with a joke? You have heard some of them like "the duck in the bar" or "the pope on the golf course." If they get laughs, they're polite laughs out of respect or sympathy for the speaker.

Recently I heard a graduation speech at Yale Law School. A professor with unchallenged recognition for her expertise in the field rattled off six jokes about lawyers that we had heard at least once before. She debased her own credentials. She diminished her own authority. An opening "funny" story is like putting on a funny hat or funny tie for a laugh. It can strip you of the respect you need to have your opinions respected.

Churchill, John Kennedy, Douglas MacArthur, Martin Luther King, Jr., and Franklin Roosevelt did not begin by telling a joke. That's not to say they didn't have a sense of humor. Churchill, FDR, and JFK had a wicked sense of humor, which they wielded with devastating results.

The problem is that many who lack either the wit of a

Churchill or the timing of a Carson think they can be stand-up comics and so embarrass themselves and their audience.

I write speeches for many CEOs. Sometimes these CEOs call me for a joke. (I did once write a book called *Podium Humor*.)

"Humes," they say on the phone, "I need a joke, you know, break the ice, to relax the audience." If they need a joke, it is to relax not the audience but themselves. It is their own antsy nerves fix.

Some executives tell me that they have a joke they've used on countless occasions. "It's a riot," they say. "Fine," I reply, "if you must use it, save it until the middle of the speech." Why? Because jokes, like praise, are not expected in the middle of the talk. As Aristotle said, "The secret of humor is surprise."

Later in the book I will tell how to turn jokes into humor, but for now I want you to concentrate on your *prime time moment*—the moment after introduction.

Pregnant Pause

Churchill said he counted to ten to let the murmur in the audience still to a dramatic silence. Then he forced himself to stand silent for a few moments more. (Sometimes to make myself stand quiet for those extra moments, I think of the Phillies' opening day World Series lineup in 1980.)

Do the same. Stand there silently until the audience thinks you may have some speech impediment. And

then—wham!—wow the people with an opening zinger!
That is the language of leadership.

The Five-Star General

After that "pregnant pause," try igniting the audience
with a choice quotation: "John Kennedy once said . . ."
"It was Vince Lombardi who said . . ."

When you are choosing a quotation, think of today's
general, who has to keep his weight down to meet Pentagon physical guidelines. His stars show his rank, and his
waist shows his fitness. The right quotation does the same.
The author of the quote should be someone you've heard
of, who commands respect and attention, not some dusty
historian or some obscure economics professor.

Yet you don't want a fat quotation that rambles on for
a paragraph or so. Pare it to one sentence—or two at the
very most.

Sensational Saga

Try beginning with a believe-it-or-not case history from
your own company's files or even a business story clipped
out of a trade association article or *The Wall Street Journal*.

Open by saying, "The head of a top trucking company
came to our Chicago manager last year with this problem. . . ."

RULE NUMBER ONE: STRONG BEGINNING

Pretend it's soap opera. Hook the audience in by recounting all the problems facing this executive. When you get the audience wondering just how the executive will get out of his predicament, you've created suspense.

Paint in the details so that the audience can imagine how the executive looked (his bald head or bow tie) or where the meeting took place (in the Palmer House coffee shop or in his company boardroom).

I begin my "Language of Leadership" talk to corporate groups this way: "On January 24, 1988, I laid a wreath on a grave. With me was an elderly white-haired lady. The grave belonged to Winston Churchill, and the lady with me was Churchill's former secretary. Afterward at tea in her row house near Chartwell, I asked her what it was like taking the dictation for Churchill's Dunkirk speech in 1940. . . ."

There is no better beginning than a story from your own experience.

The Paper Ploy

The day of the talk or the day before comb the newspapers for that offbeat story or sharp quotation that can launch your talk. The best is a news item, like a report of a new invention or a new teenage fad.

Or take a glance at the editorials or the op-ed columns for a line that is punchy but not pompous.

Don't forget the sports pages. I've heard a speaker begin with a sportswriter's description of O. J. Simpson dodging would-be tacklers that set the stage for a discussion of looming industrial problems. On another occasion I heard a speaker begin by quoting a writer's snappy recounting of a double play. It introduced a talk on unity and teamwork.

Would you believe I've even heard some accomplished speakers open with advice from "Dear Abby" or even from the horoscope for the day?

For maximum effect, brandish the newspaper before you begin, and then read from it.

The Zinger Beginner

Invent your own quotable line or zinger. Aim for shock or humor impact.

Winston Churchill began speaking to the U.S. Congress in 1941: "I can't help but reflect that if my father had been American and my mother English instead of the other way around [pause] I might have got here on my own!"

I wrote for GOP National Chairman William Brock in 1978: "The Republican Party has before it its greatest opportunity of the century [pause] *unless we blow it!*"

British Prime Minister Margaret Thatcher when she spoke to our Congress in 1984 opened: "It is said in our Parliament that when you want a bill to be introduced you go to a man, but if you want a bill to be passed [pause] you go to a woman."

On May 10, 1990, I gave a one-man show at the White House celebrating the fiftieth anniversary of Churchill's first day as prime minister. How did Churchill begin his

RULE NUMBER ONE: STRONG BEGINNING

opening speech to the House of Commons as prime minister, the equivalent of an inaugural address: "I have nothing to offer but blood, toil, tears and sweat."

That was no opening amenity! Churchill knew the language of leadership.

SIR WINSTON'S RULE NUMBER TWO: ONE THEME

. . . .

In May 1990 I stayed at the Carlton Club in London (which incidentally was blown up a couple of weeks later). This is the Conservative party club where portraits of Edmund Burke, Benjamin Disraeli, and Winston Churchill stare down from the wall. I ordered sherry trifle for my dinner dessert. The reason I ordered the sponge cake pudding was that I remembered an incident in the same club involving the same dessert. Churchill had called out to a Carlton Club waiter: "Pray, take away this pudding; it has no theme."

Well, Churchill liked his presentations—as well as his puddings—to hold together, to have one theme.

When I was a young man in the Pennsylvania legislature, I didn't know of Churchill's advice. I would address the local Kiwanis Club on the recent legislative session and talk about H.R. 1066 (the community college bill), S. 421 (the unemployment compensation bill), or H.R. 42 (a tax bill). It wasn't a speech, it was a laundry list. I would have done a lot better if I had stuck to one theme (education, business, or taxes) and then saved comment on the other subjects for the Q & A.

In 1954 the eighty-year-old prime minister came to Washington. At the Mayflower Hotel Churchill listened to an address by a ranking American political leader. After the talk the American said to Churchill: "Sir Winston, you are the greatest speaker in the world. I'd appreciate any advice about my talk."

"In all candor," Churchill replied, "the impact of your talk was [pause] underwhelming. You spoke of NATO, the need for reciprocity in trade, the importance of the Anglo-American alliance, but it had no theme."

RULE NUMBER TWO: ONE THEME

A Speech Is
Like a Symphony

Churchill knew that you may have two or three points in your talk, but the points have to come under one heading. To an associate he compared a speech with a Beethoven symphony. "A speech is like a symphony. It can have three movements, but it must have one dominant melody: dot, dot, dot . . . dah," Churchill said as he hummed the chords of Beethoven's Fifth.

Think of the songwriter. He first works out the refrain before he writes the different verses that follow the refrain.

Bottom Line

At the Smithsonian Institution in Washington (I was a Woodrow Wilson fellow at the Center for International Scholars) I once heard former Prime Minister Harold Macmillan speak. He told of his maiden address in 1922. Afterward he asked Churchill, who he said was "like an uncle," how he had done.

"Harold," Churchill harrumphed, "everyone in the gallery was saying 'Young Macmillan is giving his maiden address.' And they asked, 'what is it about?' Harold, if people can't say in one sentence what the speech is about, it's a speech not worth delivering."

An Eisenhower speech writer once gave me similar advice when he said, "Humes, you have to be able to write your theme on the back of a matchbook."

What Is the QED?

The first President I ever had real contact with was Dwight Eisenhower. I know the image of Eisenhower was that he was a genial man who wasn't too bright. Wrong! When you worked with Eisenhower, he was a five-star general, you were a private, and he and you knew the difference.

After he looked at one talk that we speech writers gave him, he banged his glasses on the Oval Office desk and barked, "What is the QED?"

Like others, I didn't associate Eisenhower with geometry.

To our puzzled looks, he thundered, "QED—*quod erat demonstrandum?* What's the bottom line? What is the message you want the audience to take away with them? What is it you want them to do? If you don't know that, you're wasting my goddamn time!"

In fact, Churchill suggested writing out the bottom line first. Write out in one sentence—before you start preparing your remarks—the message you want to leave with your listeners, so that you focus on that message, so that your talk reinforces that message.

As a onetime presidential speech writer for Gerald Ford, I was asked to help in the writing of his memoirs. Ford was thinking of the title *Straight from the Shoulder*. I said, "Mr. President, why not use the words of Solomon in Ecclesiastes? You healed the wounds of Watergate, war, and a feverish economy. Why not pick the title *Time to Heal*?

"Then, when a reader finishes each chapter, Mr. President, whether it's Jerry Ford as Eagle Scout, Jerry Ford as freshman congressman, Jerry Ford as minority leader, he will say to himself, 'Jerry Ford was a "mediator," Jerry Ford was a "reconciler," Jerry Ford was a "healer." ' "One theme!

Don't ramble from point to point. Tie up the points into one theme, be it a word like "marketing" or a sentence like "You've got to know your customer."

Don't Detour

You might not know that Churchill in addition to being a statesman, a writer, an artist, a soldier—was a sportsman. He owned racehorses. In 1949 he thought he had a winner in his black stallion Colonist II.

Before each race Churchill would go to the stable and try to inspire his steed the way he had the British people in their sternest hour.

As he patted Colonist II on the backside, he said, "If you win today, it will be your last race. You can retire to stud. Think of all that agreeable female company. Imagine those verdant pastures replete with nubile, lissome fillies hearkening and attending to every physical need."

That afternoon Colonist II, out of a field of twenty, placed nineteenth! When Churchill was asked what happened, he replied, "When I told Colonist what he could look forward to, he couldn't keep his mind on the race!"

Stick to the Theme

Well, to make a winning talk, you must make sure not to let the audience be sidetracked from the main message. If you have something to say that doesn't fit the central theme, save it for the Q & A and then wedge it into one of your answers.

Pick the message, and don't meander. You have a destination to reach; don't take a detour. You may have three points, just as you may chart different routes by car, railroad, or airplane, but you have one destination—one theme.

Churchill had read in Aristotle's *Rhetoric* that the most important thing in making a speech is keeping to one theme. Churchill agreed because he found out that if you wanted to get your audience to do something, you should not confuse it with instructions on a lot of different subjects. Keep hammering at one note.

In the 1930's Churchill told the British people to arm, rebuild the navy, reinstate the draft, develop the RAF. He didn't clutter up the message with a discussion about the weakness of the League of Nations or the provisions of the Treaty of Versailles. He kept to one theme: "Arm."

To stick to a single theme may not be as simple as it sounds. One easy way is the Dale Carnegie School solution. The instructors tell classes: "Tell the audience what you are going to say. Say it. Then tell them what you've said."

To my graduate students at the University of Pennsylvania who found it hard to wrap up their points into one theme, I gave these tips for wrapping up their talks into nice *square* little packages.

Statement of
bottom-line
message:

Before you write out notes for a talk, write out your central theme.

Quotation:

Pick a quotation that reinforces one theme (Lee Iacocca on marketing, or John Naisbitt on *Megatrends 1990*).

Umbrella:

If you have two or three different points, work up an "umbrella" word or phrase that covers all of them.

Anecdote:

Find a case story from your own company files or from your own personal experience that describes the central problem or bottom-line message.

Repetition:

Repeat at least once the bottom-line message or central theme.

Ending:

Make sure the bottom-line message is in your closing.

SIR WINSTON'S
RULE NUMBER
THREE:
SIMPLE
LANGUAGE

. . . .

Dashes and
Dot, Dot, Dots

One day, as Churchill sat down to preside over a Cabinet meeting in 10 Downing Street, he looked over at his foreign secretary, Anthony Eden, who was reading over a speech he was going to give that evening.

"It's a bad speech, Anthony," growled Churchill.

"How can you tell, Prime Minister?" replied Eden. "Surely you can't read upside down."

"I can tell," answered Churchill, "because there are no dashes [– –] and dot-dot-dots [. . .]. A speech without dashes and dot-dot-dots is an article, not a speech!"

Conversational

Churchill thought a speech should look like a radio script, not a newspaper article. It should sound the way you talk, not like some term paper you once wrote or a magazine article you recently read.

The language of leadership is simple language, conversational language. Churchill spoke on the platform as he did in conversation. Once after he spoke, some nit-picking bureaucrat confronted him and pontificated, "Prime Minister, I was very shocked that in your speech you actually terminated a sentence with a preposition."

Churchill replied, "That is pedantic nonsense . . . up . . . with which . . . I shall not put."

Franklin Roosevelt also spoke the language of leadership. During World War II some bureaucrat presented to him in the Oval Office the replica of the placard to be put on the thousands of federal office building doors. Then the GS-18 read out the sign for FDR's approval. "It is obligatory to extinguish all illumination before the premises are vacated."

A disgusted Roosevelt roared back, "Why the hell can't you say, 'Put out the lights when you leave'?"

53
· · ·

RULE NUMBER THREE: SIMPLE LANGUAGE

Tom Brokaw of NBC Nightly News once asked me what my job was like as a White House speech writer. I replied, "I'm a translator. Not French into English, but the bureaucratic into the poetic, the legalistic into the eloquent, the corporatese into the conversational, the complex into the simple."

You see, a White House speech writer is often handed a draft speech on taxes written by the deputy assistant secretary of the treasury or a speech on defense by someone in the Pentagon. I remember one time I had to "translate" a speech about mass transit from someone in the Department of Transportation. The bureaucrat's draft kept referring to "mobile demographics." I called him up and said, "Look, I'm stupid. What does that mean?"

He replied, "How people get to work."

So that's what I wrote.

General Eisenhower once handed over a speech he had written for Churchill's comments. Churchill told Eisenhower, "Dwight, the speech has too many 'zeds' and passives."

The "zeds" referred to what Americans call zees, and Churchill was objecting to Ike's use of "finalize," "prioritize," "systematize." Churchill would say, "end up," "speed up," or "plan." Churchill preferred the one-syllable Anglo-Saxon to the polysyllabic Latinate.

Pale Passives

Churchill also disliked Ike's overuse of the passive voice. In 1940 at the time of Dunkirk, when Britain's back was against the wall, Churchill delivered his historic words "[W]e shall fight on the beaches, we shall fight on the landing grounds, we shall fight in the fields and in the streets, we shall fight in the hills; we shall never surrender."

When Franklin Roosevelt heard these words in his office at the White House, he said to his aide Harry Hopkins, "As long as that old bastard is in charge, Britain will never surrender. It's not like giving to the French, which is only pouring money down the rathole."

Because of Churchill's words, Roosevelt, the head of a neutral nation, sent aid to a beleaguered Britain.

Leaders Are Not Passive

But what if Churchill had said, "Hostilities will be engaged on the coastal perimeter." Do you think America would have sent aid?

Too many Americans—maybe because they learned the passive two grades after they learned the active voice— think it sounds sophisticated.

The passive is not the voice of a leader. The passive is the voice of the bureaucrat who wants to duck responsibility. ("The policy will be implemented.") The leader says, "Let's do it!"

"Passives" rob a talk of life and action. They turn the colorful words of conversation into the pale gray of "governmentese."

RULE NUMBER THREE: SIMPLE LANGUAGE

Toss Out the Turtles

Almost as bad as the passive is the "It is necessary." Worse is "It is obligatory." If the passive is a "turtle" because the head retracts into a shell, refusing to risk exposure, its cousin is the tortoise. Martin Luther King did not say, "It is necessary to establish those rights." He said, "We shall overcome."

Don't say, "It is necessary to increase sales." Say, "We have to increase sales." I heard a CEO intone, "It is obligatory to find new markets." He should have said, "We've got to find new markets."

Toss out the tendentious turtles and pick up your pace.

Pontifical Terms

John Kennedy campaigning in 1960 said, "We want to be first—not first 'if,' not first 'but,' but first. . . ." He didn't say, "Not first, however." Samuel Pepys, the English writer, didn't end his diary entry each night with "And therefore to bed." He wrote: "And so to bed."

In conversation you don't tell a colleague, *"Therefore,* let's try direct mailing." You say, *"So* let's try direct mailing."

You don't say, "Television advertising is the best way to improve sales. *However,* it's expensive." You say, *"But* it's expensive."

You don't tell a friend, "Luigi's the best Italian restaurant in town. Moreover, it's cheap." You say, "What's more, it's cheap."

"Therefore," "however," "notwithstanding," "inasmuch," "nevertheless" are the pettifoggers' terms that belong to contracts, not to conversation. Don't weigh down your talk by pompous terms. Lighten up your delivery with the one-syllable equivalents: "so," not "therefore"; "but," not "however"; "still," not "nevertheless."

Is *Not* It Romantic?

That's not the way Frank Sinatra sang it! Speakers, like songwriters, ought to use contractions. *Contractions are conversational.* The more conversational you are, the less contrived you seem. *Those who sound stilted and stuffy don't sell their ideas.* Some of the greatest lines in history that inspired men were contractions: "Don't tread on me!" or "Don't give up the ship!"

"God Bless 'Our Local Accommodation Unit' "

Churchill once said, "The jargon of socialism is almost as bad as socialism itself. They do not speak of 'the poor.' No, they say 'marginal stipend maintainers.' They do not talk of 'house' or 'home.' No, it's 'local accommodation unit.' I suppose the Socialists will soon requisition those old samplers our grannies knitted and change them to read 'God bless our local accommodation unit."

Businessmen as well as bureaucrats often talk as if they were paid by the syllable. I heard a hospital administrator say on the *Today* show: "This operation has reduced the number of negative outcomes." Should we change the psalm to read, "Yea, though I walk in the shadow of a negative outcome"?

How many times before a threatened strike have you heard a negotiator intone on television, "We will engage in a meaningful dialogue"? Wouldn't you be more hopeful if he had said, "We're going to sit down and talk."

The favorite phrase of businessmen and bureaucrats is "interface." Doesn't that sound like something you'd want to do with Madonna or Richard Gere?

Too many yuppy executives talk as if M.B.A. stood for "Master of Bulls—Abstractions."

Get Personal

Olivia Newton-John belted out her song "Get Physical." Speakers should make their slogan "Get personal."

Use the personal pronoun "we" instead of the noun "management," "you" instead of "employees." If you want to sell your listeners, talk to them, not *at* them. When you use the third-person "front office" and "the sales force" instead of "we" and "you," you're talking not only *at* your audience but *down* to them. The magic words of speaking as well as selling are "we" and "you."

But don't use "I" to recite accomplishments or give instructions.

I heard General Eisenhower once say that Douglas MacArthur suffered from an "eye" problem. I wondered if it was glaucoma or a detached retina. Then Ike added, "The general had a fatal addiction to the perpendicular pronoun." If you use "I" to get things done, get five stars on your shoulder first because then you don't have to convince, only command.

To put persuasion in your pleas, use the personal pronouns "we" and "you."

Best Words Are the Shortest

Mark Twain once told of a Missouri farmer who ran five times for the state legislature without winning. It wasn't because he didn't practice his speeches. He practiced his campaign talks every day while milking. He referred to himself as "your humble aspirant." He referred to his audiences as "my enlightened constituents." He talked of "obtaining a mandate" for his "legislative mission."

Then one day even his cow balked at his speeches and kicked him in the teeth.

With his front teeth knocked out, the farmer could speak only words of one syllable. The result was he won his next election and kept getting reelected.

The farmer found out the hard way the language of leadership.

Banish the "Bureaucratic"

Churchill when he became the first Lord of the admiralty in World War I sent a letter to the *Oxford English Dictionary* saying "aeroplane" should be replaced by "airplane" and "hydroplane" by "seaplane." He even invented a new and simpler word for what was then called a light search and destroy vessel: "destroyer."

Churchill hated the beat-around-the-bush language of the military or CIA bureaucrats who refer to "dead and wounded" as "inoperative field personnel" or mask the word "kill" by saying "terminate with prejudice."

What if Churchill in 1940 when he was prime minister had said, "I have nothing to offer but sanguinary fluids, sudorific secretions, and lachrymal elements." Would those Latinate polysyllables have rallied his nation?

In World War I, before America entered the conflict, Churchill went on a speaking tour to promote support for British bonds. At a reception in Richmond, a woman of Rubenesque proportions hosted a reception at which wine and cold fried chicken were served.

Churchill advanced to the table and said, "I think I'd like a breast."

"Mr. Churchill," the voluptuous Virginian cooed, "nice people don't use that word for that part of the anatomy. We say 'white meat.' "

THE SIR WINSTON METHOD

The next day Churchill brought flowers for his hostess, specifically a corsage. On the corsage he affixed his card, "Winston Churchill, M.P.," to which he added his note: "I would be most obliged if you would pin this corsage on your white meat."

SIR WINSTON'S RULE NUMBER FOUR: PICTURES

. . . .

The greatest speech the British statesman ever gave he delivered in America. Why was it the greatest? Because a single speech convinced Americans to act. A single speech triggered a change in American feelings about the Soviet Union, our wartime ally, and started the Americans to rearm.

How did this single speech do it? Mainly by a single phrase.

The irony is that the phrase was not in the advance copy of the text that was sent out by the British Embassy in Washington. Churchill was staying there before embarking on a special train to Missouri with President Truman for a speaking appearance at Westminster College.

In 1946 Churchill was a defeated man. He had lost the prime ministership a year before. Churchill worried that he could not convince Americans that Soviet troops in Central and Eastern Europe were suppressing freedom— particularly when he had lost his authority as Britain's elected leader.

Draw a Picture in the Listener's Mind

He knew he had to describe in graphic, vivid language what was happening to countries like Poland, Czechoslovakia, and others. Words like "Soviet imperialism," "militarism," and "tyranny" came to mind, but such words, thought Churchill, were "abstractions." To Churchill "abstractions" were shapeless words that go in one ear and out—because they don't paint a picture in the listener's mind.

In his stateroom, as the train carrying the presidential entourage hurtled westward through the night of March 2, Churchill studied his map of Europe. His pen drew a black line from the Baltic Sea through Poland down through the

Balkans to the Adriatic Sea. He retraced that line as he
tried to think of the right picture to describe Soviet sup-
pression of rights. Around 2:00 A.M., as the train stopped
in Salem, Illinois, for refueling, Churchill looked at the
curtain dividing the sleeping part from the rest of the
stateroom.

Inspiration—perhaps from the ghost of Lincoln—
flashed, and he wrote down on his copy of the speech a few
lines in ink.

The next day in the gymnasium at Westminster College
he read from those notes: "From Stettin in the Baltic to
Trieste in the Adriatic an iron curtain has descended across
the continent."

That *picture phrase* would galvanize America and the free
world into action; the Truman Doctrine, the Marshall
Plan, and NATO followed.

What Stinks Is Not
Pollution but a Dead Fish!

Pictureless phrases like "delivery of services," "undercapitalization," "upscale marketing" do not really register in
the listener's ear unless they're reinforced by an analogy, an
anecdote, or a case example from your own business experience or company files.

Let's say you're giving a talk against pollution. You
should talk about taking your boy to a favorite fishing
stream upstate and how the lad pulled in a whopper of a

trout—and that it was bloated, yellowish, and rotten with stink. That's pollution!

But you say you don't have a son or even a friend who fishes. Well, imagine one. Make up a story. Don't worry, as long as you're not hurting anyone with your tale, it's acceptable.

Jesus Made Up Stories

Jesus Christ did. He made up stories we call parables such as the good Samaritan in the New Testament. Did you ever realize Christ never used the words "salvation," "grace," and "redemption" in his talks. No, he talked about a young man who blew his wad on wine, women, and song and then came back and said, "Dad, give me a second chance."

There was no documented case history of the wild spender. Jesus used the rabbinical or talmudic method of telling a story or an example to prove a point.

Paul in his epistles, or letters, tossed *out* such abstractions as "salvation." Such pictureless abstractions—without an image to reinforce them—may suffice in letters or articles but not in talk.

Why were Christ's words remembered fifty years later, when Gospel writers collecting material for the New Testament talked to those illiterate farmers and fishermen who had heard Christ's sermons? Because his preaching carried parables or pictures.

By the way, for you businessmen one of those parables was about private enterprise. Remember the story about the employer who before going off on a journey to a far country gave coins (talents) to his employee for safekeeping. When the employer came back and asked for the money, the employee said, "I buried it right in the ground, master." And the man was fired because he hadn't put the money to good use; he hadn't invested it!

IRAs

Aristotle in his *Rhetoric* wrote that one of the hardest things for a speaker is to come up with the analogy or picture word. It may be hard if you're trying to wax poetic, but too many speakers don't try to dig first right in the backyard of their own experiences.

The first assignment I give to my graduate students at the University of Pennsylvania is "Establish your IRAs." I don't mean a savings account even if it does entail storing away some capital that will bring eventual returns. My IRAs stand for "incident recorded accounts." Everyone in his or her own life has the unused capital of experiences, and I ask each student to write down ten incidents. Think of the stories you've often told your friends and family:

- When you almost drowned at camp

- How you met your mate on a blind date

- When your grandfather died

"Don't write out the whole story," I tell my students. "Just caption each one with a title."

THE SIR WINSTON METHOD

At the next class I tell them how each of their stories may be adapted to paint a picture analogy for some fuzzy concept.

Lack of Research: Checking out the tide first might have warned you against swimming.

The Opening of Unexpected Markets: The serendipitous meeting of a spouse.

Failure of Communication: You wished you had told your grandfather how much you appreciated and loved him.

When you recount some personal experience in a talk, you come alive because you're talking about something that happened to you. And you tell it well because you've already told it many times before.

Take a sheet, or even use the inside of this book. Write the numbers 1 to 10 down the side. Then force yourself to think of some experiences, and jot them down. Don't worry about how they can be adapted to something like planning, leverage buyout, or cost-effectiveness.

Each time you give a talk you will look at this list and find that at least one of them will suggest a picture analogy for your talk.

In the 1930's Churchill was angry at his fellow members of Parliament who were looking the other way as the Nazis consolidated their power. If his own Conservative party consisted of appeasers, the other party, the Labour, was pacifist.

He dug into his own file and related his boyhood experience to the House of Commons: "When I was a child my nanny used to take me every May to the Barnum and Bailey Circus. But there was one side show I was never allowed to look at. She said, 'Winston, it's too revolting a spectacle for the human eye.'

"It was called 'the boneless wonder.' And now after all these years where do I finally see this freak show? Not in a circus but in the House of Commons—and all around me 'the Boneless Wonders.' "

P-I-C-T-U-R-E-S

What if you find the experiences you listed don't quite fit the main talking point? Well, I'll give you the code I give to students to unlock the computer bank that is memory: P-I-C-T-U-R-E-S. You can write that down on another inside book page.

Parents:	What did your father tell you as you went off to college? Did your mother ever scold you for a messy room?
Interests:	How do you refinish a cherry table? What was your biggest find in collecting baseball cards?
Chores:	What about some stories about your teenage newspaper route or mowing lawns for neighbors?

Television:	Think of a television show or movie you watched. Think of what Gleason or Archie Bunker said. I've heard a speaker quote Clint Eastwood's "Make my day" to talk about new business competition. Another speaker re-created Gable's "Frankly, my dear, I don't give a damn!" Listeners can easily picture Eastwood or Gable.
University:	Why did a professor flunk you on an economics exam? Who was the teacher you remember best, and what were some of her or his favorite sayings?
Recreation:	In high school football what play broke the other team's defense and why? In golf how do you set up a shot?
Environment:	What about the time you went to Florida and it was close to freezing? Or talk about that major presentation when your clothes were soaked by a downpour as you went to the meeting.
Shopping:	What did your wife say when you returned from the store but left the shopping list at home?

RULE NUMBER FOUR: PICTURES

You can't see how a boyhood chore like mowing the lawn could relate to a business strategy? Well, Richard Nixon as President used it to describe détente. "In mowing a lawn you start at the edges and work to the center." In other words, Nixon said, you begin with fringe disputes such as fishing rights before you get to the core problems of arms control.

Franklin Roosevelt in arguing for the lend-lease aid to Great Britain in 1940 said, "Who of you, if you saw your neighbor's house on fire, would not lend him your hose to put out the fire?"

That is the language of leadership.

Take a Hike

If you still can't think of the right analogy, take a walk. Woods, streams, mountains all suggest ideas. Lincoln did this once. When he came across a stream, he pictured his argument for reelection. "It is not best to swap horses in the middle of the stream."

In 1953 Stalin died and Churchill wanted to advance the idea of a Big Three diplomatic negotiation. The mountains of Morocco where he vacationed gave him an inspiration.

In a speech later Churchill said, "I call for a parley at the summit." "Summit," "summit conference"—the picture gripped the world's mind as "iron curtain" had years earlier.

Go to the Zoo

Churchill loved animals. He had a standard poodle named Rufus and a cat named Marmalade, both buried at Chartwell, his country home. At one time he even kept a pet lamb that roamed the rooms of Chartwell. Outside his house two pet geese patrolled his pond. At the London Zoo he would sometimes go and feed a lion given to him that appropriately was named Winston.

To stretch his memory, Churchill let his mind wander zoologically. Churchill denounced Lady Astor and her pro-German followers as appeasers once in a House of Commons talk, saying, "An appeaser is one who feeds the crocodile hoping it will eat him last."

The barb so stung Nancy Astor that when he came a few days later to a dinner party she was hosting, she said, while pouring coffee, "Winston, if I were your wife, I'd put poison in your coffee."

And Churchill shot back, "And if I were your husband, Nancy, I'd drink it."

Paint a Picture

Animals immediately plant pictures in the mind. Secretary of the Treasury Don Regan at a time of sluggish economy in 1981 was going to say that the economy despite some outward signs showed latent strengths. I suggested to him the image of a sleeping bull.

So if your imagination suffers a rainout, do a Noah.

RULE NUMBER FOUR: PICTURES

Start counting your animals. An elephant can describe a cumbersome conglomerate; a squirrel, the need for savings; a pigeon, delivery of service; a setter dog, pinpointing a goal target; a cat, adaptability or mobility.

By the way, you don't have to shrink these animals into a one-sentence throwaway. Puff them into paragraphs. Make up an anecdote as Aesop did two thousand years ago with his fables about foxes and his tales about turtles.

Churchill's career in Parliament spanned sixty-four years. When he ran for his seat the last time in 1959, papers speculated that he was too feeble to make a speech but would probably just acknowledge the crowd's cheers with a *V*-sign wave.

That election year the issue was private enterprise. The out-of-power socialists promised nationalization of key coal, steel, and transportation industries. Their vigorous challenge brought them even with the Conservatives in the polls.

At Woodford, the London suburb that Churchill represented in Parliament, a crowd gathered around a speaker's platform draped with the Union Jack. The aged statesman sat slumped in a chair with a blanket covering his legs from the October chill. When he was introduced, the onlookers wondered whether he could even rise from his chair. He did—with difficulty—and spoke at first faintly but then gathering in power: "Let the last appearance in my not uneventful parliamentary career be a testament to private enterprise"—and here Churchill pointed his cane like a gun—"as a tiger, a predatory animal to be shot." Then Churchill crouched slightly and pumped his hands in a milking notion and added, "The drones of bureaucracy see private enterprise as an old cow to be milked, but" boomed Churchill with a sweeping gesture, "you hardworking Englishmen see it as the sturdy horse pulling along the cart of democracy."

A week later the polls soared in favor of the Conservatives. The old lion had spoken for the last time. In a one-minute talk the old warrior had transformed a dry abstraction like private enterprise into a powerful picture.

SIR WINSTON'S
RULE NUMBER
FIVE:
EMOTIONAL
ENDING

. . . .

Peanut Butter
or Bergdorf Goodman?

At a seminar for corporate executives I concocted this tale:

Two men are pursuing the same young woman. The first plunks himself down beside her, hauls out his wallet, and announces, "Sugar, here's a gold American Express card, here're the keys to the BMW, here's a key to the condo, and here's the Bergdorf Goodman credit card. Will you marry me?"

The second suitor says, "Dearest, I can't offer you anything at least for the next year. I'm afraid we're going to have to live over the garage and eat peanut butter sandwiches because I'm writing the great American novel. But I can't write without you. In fact, I can't live without you. I need you. I love you."

Then I asked the executives which guy do you think she picked, the Bergdorf Goodman or the peanut butter?

Almost all the hands shot up for the Bergdorf Goodman suitor.

"Wrong!" I said. When some objected, I countered, "How many of you have children?" Again most of them raised their hands. "How do you have them," I asked, "by artificial insemination?" People respond when you tell them you need them.

The Power of Pride

When I told one CEO that a talk without feeling was flat, he said, "Look here, Humes, I'm not trying to save a country in wartime like a Churchill. I just want to deliver a message."

"Wait a minute," I answered the CEO. "Didn't I hear you a little while ago talking about your company's history, its tradition, its reputation of quality? That's pride.

RULE NUMBER FIVE: EMOTIONAL ENDING

Pride is an emotion—pride in your company, pride in your product."

Almost any talk can be ended on appeal to pride—pride in your city or community, pride in your industry (whether it be auto or air conditioners), pride in your vocation (whether you're an astronaut or accountant).

How did Churchill end one of his greatest speeches in World War II: "Let us . . . brace ourselves to our duties and so bear ourselves that if the British Empire and its Commonwealth last for a thousand years, men will still say: 'This was their finest hour.' "

Pride in country—that's how Churchill steeled the resolve of Britons during their ordeal of World War II.

Joe Paterno of Penn State or John Thompson of the Georgetown Hoyas might review some key plays in halftime, but they enforce their pitch with appeal to pride. It is not reason but passion that stirs the ear.

Any boxer will tell you that hitting in the gut (solar plexus) is better than hitting in the head.

Ronald Reagan bested Walter Mondale in the 1984 presidential debate not because he "outfacted" his Democratic opponent but because he "outfeelinged" him.

And Mike Dukakis lost his debate in 1988 with George Bush because he couldn't show feelings when asked a hypothetical question about his reaction to the mugging or rape of his wife.

When I'm asked to write speeches for political candidates as well as for CEOs, I give them this task: "I want you to think over those moments or experiences in your life that moved you close to tears."

A candidate for governor told me the recollection of his father as they circled around Ellis Island in a boat and his father recounted to him his dreams when he first sighted the Statue of Liberty as an immigrant sailing from Sicily.

A top executive of Merrill Lynch experienced the same emotions when he returned to the old homestead in Ireland and his aged aunt told him of his father's hopes for him and his brothers when they left for America.

Vision as a Force

Hope, like pride, is a powerful emotion. What is hope but a dream for the future? In almost any talk you can end by spelling out what the future will hold: the new markets that a new product will open, the new jobs a new branch office will create, the new opportunities a company reorganization or a new invention will generate.

How did Dr. Martin Luther King cap his magnificent speech on civil rights in 1963? "I have a dream that one day . . ." The memorial before which King spoke had engraved on it Lincoln's own words of hope a century earlier "that this nation under God shall have a new birth of freedom. . . ."

During World War II Churchill closed a speech saying: "I see a day when men and women walk together in broad sunlit, uplands in a world undimmed by bigotry and fear."

What's a more powerful emotion than pride or hope? Love: love of God, love of country—two feelings that Ronald Reagan tapped in his speech closings.

RULE NUMBER FIVE: EMOTIONAL ENDING

I once drafted a speech for Margaret Thatcher when she was Conservative leader of the opposition in 1975. The instruction from the central party office was "Be sure to mention God and queen because the socialists can't bring themselves to mention either one."

Daniel Webster closed his most famous oration with "Liberty and Union, now and forever, one and inseparable."

General MacArthur speaking to the West Point cadets in 1962 ended by saying, "My last thoughts will be the Corps, the Corps, the Corps."

If some politicians on the left sometimes shy from dwelling on love of country, they do like to end on "love of humanity," thus reaching out to the downtrodden and forgotten.

One executive said to me, "I can see how I might end a talk on a note of pride or hope, but love of country seems too purple-passioned for my ordinary business talk."

I replied, "Why not try love of family?"

You've Gotta Have Heart

A savings and loan company in Philadelphia advertised for ten years "Put a little love away."

Computer companies that bring libraries to a child's room: *That's love of family*. Insurance companies that provide security and health to home and dear ones: *That's love of family*.

THE SIR WINSTON METHOD

Frank Sinatra sang "You've gotta have heart." Well, the language of leadership is the language of heart.

If you find it hard to express those feelings from the heart, borrow from a songwriter or, better yet, a poet.

Kennedy did. He ended speeches in 1960 quoting Robert Frost:

But I have promises to keep,
And miles to go before I sleep,
And miles to go before I sleep.

Churchill did. Referring to U.S. aid, he closed a talk with lines from Arthur Clough that ended: "But westward, look, the land is bright."

Churchill who liked to begin strongly liked to end strongly, too. He often did that by closing his address with some poetry or a poignant personal story.

Do you remember how often President Reagan in his speeches to Congress would point to some doer of a heroic act in the gallery: a rescuer of passengers from a crushed plane or a community volunteer who takes meals to shut-ins.

Don't say you don't know of anyone who's done anything particularly inspiring. Call the local Scout Council, United Fund office, or the city editor of the local newspaper.

For business heroics check the in-house company bulletin or the trade association sheet for announcements of achievement. Then build around a triumph. Describe the person as well as the mountain she or he scaled. To build a little suspense, pull a Reagan and don't reveal his or her name until the very end.

RULE NUMBER FIVE: EMOTIONAL ENDING

On one occasion Churchill closed a speech with both a personal experience and a poem. In June 1941, when Britain still stood alone, Churchill delivered an address that was beamed to America:

A few weeks ago I received a letter from President Roosevelt and in it was a poem by Longfellow—written in his own handwriting which he said applied to your people as it does to us:

Sail on, O Ship of State
Sail on, O Union, strong and great!
Humanity with all its fears
With all its hopes of future years
Is hanging breathless on thy fate!

Then he added:

What is the answer that I shall give in your name? Here it is:
Give us the tools and we will finish the job.

Well, in a sense Churchill offered five tools for the language of leadership, so you could do your job on the rostrum!

1. Begin with a zinger.

2. Stick to one theme.

3. Keep the words short and sweet.

4. Paint a picture.

5. End with emotion.

Eleven

THE
SPEECH-A-MATIC

. . . .

E-A-S-E

About ten years ago while transferring planes at O'Hare Airport in Chicago, I heard a voice: "Mr. Humes, Mr. Humes, Ease, E-A-S-E, exemplify, amplify, specify, electrify."

It was one of my former students, and he shouted, as we passed on people-movers in different directions, the acronym for preparing a short talk.

Are you worried about making a short talk or presentation when you have no time to prepare? Relax! This instant speech formula writes it for you. It's so simple, it's EASE-Y!

Let's imagine that you're on a commuter train or even eating at the business luncheon head table. Pull out an old envelope, and write vertically on it:

EXEMPLIFY

AMPLIFY

SPECIFY

ELECTRIFY

Now the crucial step to this easy formula is filling the space beside EXEMPLIFY.

In most short talks or presentations you are recommending a program or plan of action. In short, you are suggesting a solution to a problem.

Let's say the problem is bad marketing, runaway costs, or poor research. What you have to do is come up with a case story that exemplifies the problem.

Figure out a scenario that exemplifies the bad marketing problem. It could be that upscale yuppies aren't going into the five-and-ten.

If you want an example about runaway costs, call the auditing department and check out that rumor that employees hired limos on certain occasions instead of taking cabs.

To dramatize the need for better research, show how a

survey could have indicated that wives, not their husbands, choose the underarm deodorant.

Or let's say your company has volunteered your services to the United Fund or Boy Scout drive. Call the local headquarters. It'll give you plenty of material. Maybe it's a story about a junior high school basketballer from the ghetto who was burned in a tenement fire and how the Burn Foundation—supported by the United Fund—made it possible for that young man to play again when right after the accident doctors said he wouldn't ever walk again.

Exemplify

"Exemplify" is another way of saying "paint a picture." Draw a picture in the listener's mind of that yuppie buyer, the stretch limo, or the housewife shopper.

Amplify

"Amplify" just means expanding on the problem you described in "Exemplify." In the space besides AMPLIFY you can list other mini examples. For instance, in the United Fund talk, you could mention other activities supported by the fund; how a test for glaucoma saved an old lady's sight or how marital counseling mended a marriage.

Or next to AMPLIFY you can jot down reasons why the United Fund goal has to be met: public health, public recreation, etc. Or in the business talk for that space you can just list reasons why the present marketing is slumping, or why the big ticket costs are slipping through the audit net, or why the research department has to be updated.

Specify

"Specify" is simple. Just state the solution for the problem. In the case of the United Fund that can be the target goal. In your business presentation that's when you outline the shift you recommend for marketing or when you spell out your plan for a new research department.

Electrify

"Electrify" means to galvanize your audience into action. My schoolteacher mother told me of the little girl who wrote an essay on Benjamin Franklin. "Benjamin Franklin was born in Boston. Benjamin Franklin moved to Philadelphia. Benjamin Franklin married. Then Benjamin Franklin discovered electricity."

Well, whatever turned on Benjamin Franklin, you have to "turn on" the audience. Appeal to their community spirit or company pride. Paint the opening of new opportunities; describe the difference their time and contribution could make to just one family.

THE SPEECH-A-MATIC

For the United Fund appeal you can close by asking each of them to reach deep in their pockets for that "fair share."

When you call for a new marketing plan or a new research department, spell out the role for those in the audience: how they're all needed to make it work, how it will make their work more productive as well as more profitable (remember to use the pronouns "we" and "you").

Then close on that note of pride or hope.

Here's a sample outline for a PTA talk proposing a new traffic light.

Exemplify:	Tell the tragic story of a Westinghouse Science Fair school winner being killed at that lightless intersection.
Amplify:	Give other reasons. 1. Noise 2. Teen drivers' speedway Give another miniexample: the recent rash of bicycle accidents at that intersection.
Specify:	Reproduce the city council ordinance.
Electrify:	For love of family each should write city council.

THE MAGIC
QUOTE MAKER

....

Quotesmaster General

President Nixon once introduced me by saying, "Jamie Humes is a Walking Bartlett's, the quotesmaster general of the White House speech writers."

Actually the way I first came to the attention of the White House was not through my speech writing but through my quotes collecting.

The Sir Winston Method

Like Churchill, I had been given *Bartlett's Familiar Quotations* by my mother for my eighteenth birthday, and I delved into it, jotting down in my own notebooks the quotations that particularly inspired me.

I then filed them for speech use under the headings "Apathy," "Business," "Community," "Democracy," etc. I did this not because I wanted to be a speech writer but because I wanted to be a speech giver, a future representative or senator. In fact, I think I was the first appointment to the White House speech-writing staff whose qualifications turned on my speaking experience, not my writing.

C-R-E-A-M

As I flipped through my black-binder books of quotations, looking for the right quote (my pile reached halfway to the bedroom ceiling), I began to see that great quotes often sound much the same. Sure, the wisdom varies and the words are different, but the way the words were put together were much alike. I counted five ways to write the "quotable" quotation.

Like cream, the memorable quotations rise to the top—the tops in familiarity, notability, and memorability.

And C-R-E-A-M spells the five different ways great leaders like Winston Churchill, Franklin Roosevelt, John Kennedy, and Martin Luther King made their words memorable.

Contrast

"Contrast" is one way writers make lines memorable.

John Kennedy said: "If a free society cannot help the many who are poor, it cannot save the few who are rich."

Churchill said: "If we open a quarrel between the past and the present, we shall find we have lost the future."

Lincoln's Second Inaugural is remembered for these noble lines that begin "With malice toward none, with charity for all. . . ."

The Beatitudes in the New Testament ring with paradox and contrast. So do the Proverbs in the Old Testament. Just open a page of Benjamin Franklin's *Poor Richard's Almanack,* and you will read these antonyms in his adages:

Rich—poor

Spender—saver

Old—young

Dark—light

Mountain—valley

Present—future

Winter—summer

Rhyme

"Rhyme" is the favorite ploy of many speakers, including Jesse Jackson, to drive a message home.

Franklin Roosevelt said: "It is not a tax bill but a tax relief bill providing relief not for the *needy* but for the *greedy*."

Abraham Lincoln said in 1860: "Let us have faith that *right* makes *might*. . . ."

Richard Nixon in pushing for détente proposed: "Let us move from the era of *confrontation* into the era of *negotiation*."

John Kennedy said to Latin American diplomats in 1962: "Those who make peaceful revolution *impossible* will make violent revolution *inevitable*."

Mothers in the nursery or songwriters in Tin Pan Alley don't own a patent on rhyming. They sound them because they forever ring in the ear.

Echo

"Echo" is the word I use to describe a device favored since the days of the Greeks. Aristotle describes it in his book *Rhetoric;* it is the technique of repeating a word or phrase.

Franklin Roosevelt in his 1933 inaugural said: "The only thing we have to *fear* is *fear* itself."

Benjamin Franklin at the time of the Declaration of Independence signing cracked: "We must all *hang* together, or assuredly we shall all *hang* separately."

Churchill said of the RAF: "Never in the field of human conflict was *so* much owed by *so* many to *so* few."

Jimmy Carter in receiving the Liberty Award on July 4,

1988, in Philadelphia said: "America did not invent *human rights* but in a sense, *human rights* invented America."

No leader mastered the "echo" technique better than Kennedy: "Let us never *negotiate* out of *fear* but let us never *fear* to *negotiate*."

And his most quoted line goes: "Ask not *what your country can do for you;* ask *what you can do for your country*."

Alliteration

"**A**lliteration" may be a technique that second-rate preachers and politicians often overuse and abuse, but it does ring a bell in the memory.

Kennedy said at Amherst College in 1963: "When *power* leads man toward arrogance, *poetry* reminds him of his limitations."

Roosevelt said: "The truth is *found* when men are *free* to pursue it."

Dr. Martin Luther King in his address at the Lincoln Memorial looked to a day when people "will not be judged by the *color* of their skin, but by the *content* of their *character*."

Metaphor

"**M**etaphor" is the fifth way speakers paint a memorable line in the mind of their audience.

I have already mentioned Churchill's use of "iron curtain" and "summit." He also liked the analogy of animals:
"Dictators ride to and fro upon tigers which they dare not
dismount."

Reptiles, not mammals, were his favorite metaphors
for the Nazis. I cited the "feeds the crocodile" line earlier, but another time he used snakes: "The Nazis are
like the boa constrictors that first befoul their victim
with the filthy spray of their propaganda before they en-
gorge it."

Roosevelt in a fireside chat said of Nazi Germany in
1941: "When you see a rattlesnake poised to strike, you do
not wait until he has struck before you crush him."

Do-It-Yourself Quotes

As you read these lines of leaders, you're probably mut-
tering to yourself, "Look, I'm no Churchill or Lincoln, and
I don't have on tap the services of a fancy speech writer as
Roosevelt and Kennedy did. I can't begin to write such
lines!"

Well, my answer is that I'm not suggesting you write a
whole talk that way but just one line, one line that could
forever stay in your listeners' ears like chewing gum under
a bus seat.

You can use that line as a beginning zinger for your
speeches. Or you may want it in the middle to sound your

theme. Maybe you want to save it to the very end for your bottom-line closing.

Just try it for a single sentence. And I'll make it so simple that you'll be able to coin your own do-it-yourself quote in less time than it takes to read this chapter.

Contrast

For a contrast line write down these words to start the mind running:

Buyer—seller

Rich—poor

Ends—means

Givers—takers

Leader—follower

Lender—borrower

Up—down

Winner—loser

Then put together the contrasting words in sentences like these:

- If you can meet costs when the market is *down*, you'll make profits when it turns *up*.

- You can't lift up the *poor* by pulling down the *rich*.

- Every *leader* was first a *follower*.

- The *buyer* counts the costs, but the *seller* counts the buyers.

Rhyme

For a good rhyme line, try playing with these combinations:

Sell—tell—fell—well

Survive—thrive—strive

Buy—die—vie—try—defy

Invest—divest—best—test

Earn—learn—yearn—turn

Gain—pain—wane—retain

If those combinations don't suggest a line, do what Kennedy's speech writer Ted Sorensen did—buy a paperback rhyming dictionary.

I did when I wrote for Presidents and I found that the one syllable words were the easiest to rhyme. For the moment I toss out these quickies:

- Those who first *learned* the market are those who now have *earned* the big profits.

- All of you are going to *thrive* and prosper in next year's economy, if you can just *survive* the next few months.

- If we don't *begin* today's research, we won't *win* tomorrow's markets.

Echo

To get the echo effect, I'll reveal to you my magic formula, called the Dazzling Dozen, twelve of the simplest and oldest verbs most often used. Write them down on a sheet of paper.

Bear

Bring

Come

Get

Give

Make

Put

Reach

Sit

Stand

Take

Work

And then alongside them use these eleven adverbs:
See how a different adverb changes the meaning of these
Anglo-Saxon verbs.

- If we are to *take over* the lead in productivity, we must
  first *take out* the problem of illiteracy.

- If we don't *stand up* now to the competition, we'll no
  longer *stand out* as the leaders in the market.

Across

Down

For

In

Out

Over

To

Under

Up

With

Without

- We will *reach* our goal if we *reach out* to the upside market.

- To *hold out* in this kind of market we are first going to have to *hold down* costs.

Play with the Dazzling Dozen to devise your memorable line. It's easier than a crossword puzzle and a lot more fun.

Alliteration

Try out these amalgams for alliteration. (As you can see, I pick consonants because they have more bite than vowels.)

Business—bureaucracy—bleed—buyer—bottom (line)

Costs—cuts—concern—care—conditions—company

Goal—game—gain—guts

Money—market—means—management

Plans—programs—principles—profits

Sales—success—system—solution—score—services

Time—talk—task—test—team

- You can't *b*uild business by *b*leeding the *b*uyer.

- Even a bigger *c*ost would be to *c*ut our service.

- The problem is not lack of *m*oney but lack of *m*anagement.

· Unless we develop a *p*lan, we can forget any *p*rofits.

· This new *s*ystem will *s*ucceed because it will *s*ell!

If these words don't set your mind moving, give it a jump start by buying a *Roget's Thesaurus* or synonym book to find the right alliterative alliance of words.

Metaphor

For a memorable metaphor try the Churchill gambit of going to the zoo.

· If the cat has nine lives, the S&Ls thought they had ninety.

· We're not bees that can take from each pretty flower to make honey.

· The little ant survived for millions of years when the big dinosaur didn't. Why? Because it understood teamwork.

· The success of a company depends not on its size but on its speech and ability to maneuver. That is why the king of the jungle is not the elephant but the lion.

The Setup Punch

Ronald Reagan was the "Great Communicator," but try to think of a line you can remember by him. "There you go again" was more of an expletive, and "Make my day" came from a Clint Eastwood movie.

Yet Churchill, Roosevelt, Kennedy, and Lincoln, fill up pages in Bartlett's. Why?

Because Reagan refused to "set up" his quotable lines.

Kennedy said, "And so, *my fellow Americans* [pause], ask not what your country can do. . . ." Why did he say, "My fellow Americans"? After all, he wasn't speaking to French or Germans in his inaugural address.

Roosevelt said *"Let me again assert my firm belief* [pause] that the only thing we have to fear . . ." Why did he say, "Let me again assert my firm belief"? He wasn't insisting on his sincerity; he was introducing his zinger.

Churchill said in 1940, *"I say to you as I said to the Government last night* [pause] that I have nothing to offer you but blood, toil, tears and sweat. . . ."

All these setup lines are "magic markers"; they make what follows memorable.

Reagan had a line in his 1981 inaugural. "If we love our country, we should also love our countrymen." Here was an echo line, but he refused advice from me among others to set it up by saying, "And so, my fellow Americans, I say to you [pause] if we love our country, we should also love our countrymen."

Applause would have followed, and it would now be recorded in Bartlett's.

Why did Reagan refuse to use a setup line? Because Reagan thought such lines as "My fellow citizens," "I say to you" "And so, ladies and gentlemen," "Let me again say" sounded like a hack state senator speechifying at a courthouse rally.

And he's right that those politicians who load their speeches up with "my fellow Americans" "turn off" audiences and eventually get "turned out" of office.

But my advice is to use it only *once*! Use it only that *one time* you have a zinger line you want to fire.

The Best at the Last

One other thing: If your zinger line comes anywhere after the opening sentence, it should end a paragraph or thought. Don't lead off with a zinger line and then try to explain it. No, you explain first what the central problem or main theme is, then you set up your zinger line and unleash it.

Almost fifteen years ago during the worst of the fuel crisis I was writing a speech for the head of the major oil company. In his conversation to me about his upcoming talk he said that the problem lay not in industry but in government. "America," he said, "has three times as much fossil fuel in the ground than any of the other countries in the world. So why should Carter be pushing the panic button in alarm? He should be encouraging American companies to extract that fuel."

I played with the word "panic," but it wasn't a good word to rhyme with. But what about "scare"? I started to run through the alphabet of rhymes: "air," "bear," "care," "dare," "fair."

THE MAGIC QUOTE MAKER

I worked out a rhyming line with "dare." I didn't start out with this line. I had to lead up to it:

"The Federal government with its alternative gas days and new restrictions is spreading panic. The answer to our shortage is right in our own backyard—under the ground—if only the government will offer the right economic incentives to encourage industry to get at our oil, our coal, our natural gas.

"And so, my friends, I say to you [pause]: The time has come for the government to stop *scaring* the American people and begin *daring* them."

Use a setup line before you wield your knockout punch.

QUOTE LIKE
A LEADER

....

A head of a company who had asked me to his office to draft a speech, said, "James, I've seen some of those speeches you've written and they're top-notch or I wouldn't have invited you here, but to me they have too many quotes in them. Maybe John Kennedy," he added, "can quote from the likes of poets and philosophers, but not I. I don't read much unless it's a magazine like *Forbes* or a book like *The Peter Principle*."

Well, a leader taps into far more than he reads. And I will show you how—if you let me introduce you to the "4-H Club". To farmers the four H's stand for husbandry, health, home, heart. My grouping stands for heroes, home, history, holidays.

Heroes

When Richard Nixon was considering a presidential candidacy in 1968, he knew his greatest asset was his knowledge of foreign policy and his acquaintanceship with so many of the world leaders. He had met in his official travels statesmen such as Winston Churchill, Charles de Gaulle, Konrad Adenauer, Josip Tito, Jawaharlal Nehru among others.

As one who was contributing to the Nixon effort early I collected quotations of these leaders that might be helpful to him to refer to in his speeches.

I thought that Nixon by quoting leaders he had met was a Nixon who could deftly imply his vast experience: "I remember meeting Dr. Nehru in New Delhi and one of his favorite sayings was 'What we need is a generation of peace.' "

I don't know whether Nixon actually heard those words or not. I read them in a Nehru biography.

You can use the same technique by thinking of the great men you have met or even heard at a dinner.

Maybe you or even your father met John Kennedy. Describe the experience, and add, "And one line I particularly remember goes: 'It is time for a new generation of leadership, to cope with new problems and new opportunities.' "

Home

What famous person was born in your hometown? One steel executive told me he was born in Cresson, Pennsylvania. "It's a little town in western Pennsylvania," he said, "but the great Arctic explorer Admiral Robert Peary was born there."

For his speech I went to the library for a biography of Peary and found a quotation by the polar pioneer about planning that fitted perfectly into the executive's speech on management goals.

Another executive said to me when I asked about where he grew up, "Well, the only person I can think of who fits your category of 'famous' is Lily Tomlin. She went to the same high school though she's younger." He could say: "I'm sure a lot of you laugh at Lily Tomlin—I know I do—and I feel like I know her. She went to the same high school I did, though she was closer to my younger sister's age. One thing she said is so sad but true: "If you win the rat race, you're still a rat.' "

If you never met a President, you might share the birthday of one. A friend of mine who was born on April 13 has collected the sayings of Thomas Jefferson and always finds one that he can fit into a talk.

THE SIR WINSTON METHOD

One executive I wrote a speech for grew up in Salisbury, North Carolina, and he told me that Andrew Jackson once studied law there. His speech said: "As a boy I used to walk by the house in Salisbury where Andrew Jackson studied law before moving to Tennessee. There was one thing he said as a young captain in the War of 1812 that applies to us today: 'We are facing a test that will establish our character.' "

Most of our heroes are not politicians. My hero when I was growing up was Ted Williams. I referred to him in a speech this way: "As a boy I knew every stat of Ted Williams, and later, when I was in the Nixon White House, I got to meet him when he was manager of the Washington Senators. He said of Red Soxer Carl Yastrzemski, who eventually replaced him in the left field of Fenway Park, 'Yes, when he first came up to the Red Sox he had so much going for him that I told the coaches, "Leave him alone and let him develop by himself." And I think that is good advice for the situation today.' "

If you ever met anyone famous, buy or borrow a biography about him or her and collect a few quotes. By the way, if the celebrity is a star or singer, think of a line in the movie he made or one lyric she sang.

History

Leaders are not born; they are made. And they themselves are the makers! Presidents like Woodrow Wilson, Theodore Roosevelt, Dwight Eisenhower, and Richard Nixon read up on Julius Caesar and Napoleon as well as on Washington and Lincoln. Today Lee Iacocca's autobiography is a best seller. Why? Because businessmen want to know the secret of leadership.

One secret is that the mind of a leader never turns off. Leaders—even when they are sightseers or spectators—are active, not passive observers. Even when they are only watching, their minds are working, seeing parallels in movie plots and football plays for their own problems.

In 1976 at the Republican National Convention in Kansas City I went with a group that included a governor to the Truman museum in nearby Independence. A guide in the museum pointing to a gift from the Israeli government told of the meeting when President Chaim Weizmann was greeted by President Truman at the White House. Truman said, "I head a nation of a hundred thirty-seven million people." Weizmann replied, "Mr. President, I head a nation of a million 'presidents.' " I could see the governor writing the exchange down as a future quotation or an anecdote to explain the necessity of compromise or teamwork.

You don't have to be a historian to talk history. You have seen and heard the sights and sounds of history either as a parent or as a child when you visited the shrines of Independence Hall, Mount Vernon, Gettysburg, the Alamo, or Pearl Harbor.

Think of the visit that most impressed you and what impressed most about it. Mine that vein of that experience, and polish the nugget into a jewel of wisdom.

A friend of mine who is the head of a bank had to deliver

a civic speech. He told me that when he visited the White House with a business delegation, he was shown just outside the Oval Office an uncompleted painting entitled "The Signing of the Declaration." His talk ended this way: "I remember at the White House we were shown this unfinished portrait of the Declaration signing. President Eisenhower had the picture hung because it represented the hand of Divine Providence. You see, the artist died before he could complete it, so most of the portrait is raw unfinished canvas. But to Eisenhower that meant that all of us—not just the signers or statesmen—belong in the picture. All of us as Americans have a sworn duty to make that dream of freedom a reality."

The head of a departmental company told me of his trip to Menlo Park, New Jersey, to the laboratory of Thomas Edison. He remembered the guide recounting a reporter's interview of the great inventor when he was working to perfect the incandescent bulb. "Mr. Edison," he said, "I understand you have already suffered a hundred fifty-seven failures in your experiments."

"No," Edison replied. "I've discovered a hundred fifty-seven ways that don't work!"

Holidays

When you think of places you've visited at home, don't forget your experiences traveling abroad. Almost every country can be a source of wisdom. If you've visited Rome, you might have heard a tour guide tell you of a returning general's victorious procession through the city. The general was driven in a chariot, preceded by his marching legions, trumpeting heralds, and maybe a few elephants. Crouched in the bottom of the chariot out of sight of the crowd, a hunched man repeated in a whisper only for the general's ears. "You're only a man, you're only a man!"

If you've visited Madrid or even one of the Caribbean islands, you can tell the story of Columbus, who sailed under Queen Isabella's flag which bore the motto *Ne plus ultra,* meaning "nothing farther," which geographically described Spain's westernmost position on the Atlantic. When Columbus returned with the report of his findings, the queen ordered the *Ne* painted out to read *Plus ultra*—something more, something further—in other words, the opening of new horizons and new opportunities.

Anyone who visited London has seen St. Paul's Cathedral, which was built by Christopher Wren and was a model for our own Capitol. When the cathedral was completed in 1680, King James told Wren, "I find this cathedral awful, artificial, and amusing."

Wren replied, "I am honored by your words." That's because at that time "awful" meant "awe-inspiring," "artificial" meant "artistically made," and "amusing" meant "amazing."

I've heard one IBM speaker tell the story to point out that the word "computer" in 1950 suggested a different picture or meaning from what the word conveys today. The story is a metaphor for change. In the same way you could say the roles of lawyers, accountants, and housing developers all have changed and suggest new meanings and responsibilities.

To an executive who just came back from Germany where so many Gothic cathedrals stand, I gave this closing story: "A German philosopher once told of a passerby watching three stonemasons. He asked the first, 'What are you doing?' and he answered, 'Chipping stone.' He then questioned the second mason, and he answered, 'Building a wall.' Then he posed the question to the third, and he replied, 'I'm building a cathedral.' "

Leaders are readers! Even thousands who don't read widely read wisely. They clip out articles and turn back pages storing up lines for future use. *If you want to quote like a leader, note like a leader.*

CONFERENCE

CHARISMA

· · · · · · · · · ·

There are generally two types of committee or board meetings: one in which you have to give a report and one in which you don't.

Don't Read a Report

If you have to deliver a report, don't read it. You should know enough about your department to look your fellow board or staff members in the eyes and not look down at your typed account.

Your report should be just that, a report. A crisis analysis. Not a laundry list or a diary.

Pulling out a card from your pocket with a numbered list of items and accomplishments and droning on about each one of them in turn is not leadership.

A Laundry List Is
Not the Language of Leadership

A leader doesn't introduce each item with "And then there is the Jones and Wilson matter . . ." or "Then in April we were involved on the opening of the new branch office . . ."

Whether you're at the head table for a speech or at the conference table for a talk, you have to single out a theme.

Beam a Theme

Is there a pattern to your recent activities? Is there a plan? Is there a thrust in your accomplishments? Is there a theme? *A leader doesn't just recite; he offers an insight.* He doesn't just recite; he enlightens.

Go over your record, and try to describe in one word phrase the direction you've been heading toward. New accounts? Increased sales? Cutting costs? New products?

You're a leader, so think "general." *Generalize.*

My formula for a report is simple: Generalize, fragmentize, generalize.

I learned the report technique in a course on art history. The professor said: "First stand twenty feet away from the painting, and give your general impression. Then go up close and check on the brushwork, and the mixture of colors, and then go back twenty feet again and recap your impressions on the basis of the close-up study."

Whether you're reporting on paintings or programs, it's the same. First *generalize,* so your listeners get a general idea of the major problem you've been facing or the plan of action you have been taking.

Then *fragmentize*—that is, break it up into little pieces: *geographically* (Midwest, New England); *topically* (advertising, marketing, sales); and *chronologically* (present to future).

Finally *generalize* again. Let your listeners take away in a sentence or two what you've been striving to do or succeeded in doing.

Be a "General"

The leader is someone whose report is remembered the day after. To be a leader, be that "general." *Generalize, fragmentize* (back up your generalizations), and then *generalize* again.

The only thing worse than someone reading a report he has prepared is someone who doesn't prepare and rambles on.

THE SIR WINSTON METHOD

Too many think that if they don't have to give a report to a meeting, they don't have to prepare. Wrong!

Once Winston Churchill went by cab to a meeting. When the cab stopped at the address, Churchill delayed getting out. The Cockney driver yelled, "You 'ave arrived, governor. You're 'ere."

"I know, I know," replied Churchill. "I'm just preparing my impromptu remarks."

From the days when he first went to Parliament, Churchill never attended any meeting—be it a group conference or a private luncheon—without first organizing his thoughts into a pointed message.

Well, you ask, how did he always know what others would talk about? Shouldn't you wait to see how the discussion develops and then contribute as you see fit? No, that's laziness, not leadership.

Define the Problem

Twenty-five hundred years ago a new Chinese emperor took the throne of the Middle Kingdom. Because he was only eighteen, he called to him the court's wisest adviser.

"O learned sage, O venerable counselor, you advised my grandfather the emperor for many years. What is the single most important advice you can give for ruling my kingdom?"

And Confucius replied, "First, you must define the problem."

That is my advice to you. The day before the meeting

think of the central problem facing your company or your department. Is it rising costs, delayed deliveries, decline in service?

Take a three-by-five-inch card. On the blank side define the problem in a sentence or two. Then turn it over, and on the ruled side jot two or three recommendations.

1. Cut overhead.
    a. Eliminate consultants.
    b. Pare public relations.

2. Purchase bigger quantities.

3. Look for new suppliers.

Put the card in your pocket, and go to the meeting and wait. Don't speak up at the beginning of the meeting or your contribution will be forgotten at the end. Let others ramble. Sit back.

John Mitchell, who became attorney general under Nixon after running his 1968 presidential campaign, won Nixon's attention by his crisp summations of problems. Mitchell would smoke his pipe and look wise until the forty-five-minute mark in an hour meeting. Then he would cut off discussion with a concise analysis. "Well, we have talked about advertising, the upcoming speeches, the photo opportunity appearances, but doesn't it all boil down to what message we want to give the voters? Isn't what we're trying to say is that it's a troubled world and only Nixon has the experience to lead us?"

Israel Putnam said at the Battle of Ticonderoga, "Don't fire until you see the whites of the enemy's eyes." Well, my advice is: Don't fire until you see the eyes of others at the meeting begin to glaze. Go load up—by glancing at your three-by-five-card. Then wait until someone ends talking, and fire.

If you do that, I bet you'll be the only one who defines the problem. You'll be the only one who sounds like a leader!

Fifteen

BOFFO

INTROS

··········

A Prologue,
Not a Catalog

Most of the time I'm introduced, the introducers just wing it by reading off my résumé. Do I really want the audience to know I was born in 1934? Does the audience really care if I have two daughters? Is it necessary to hear a year-by-year recital of my career?

An introduction should be a prologue,

not a catalog that lists education and professional accomplishments. You don't build up a speaker by boring his
audience!

You want to whet the audience's interest, not weigh
them down with vital statistics. The secret of a strong
introduction is to *interest* the audience. The listeners want
more than facts; they want the flesh-and-blood personality. A good presentation paints the portrait of the
man.

Don't tie yourself to the speaker's curriculum vitae. You
must read it, of course, but then release yourself from it.

How? By following this formula: *I could say. . . , I'd
rather say. . . , What does that say . . . ?*

I Could Say

Run down the list of the speaker's achievements and pick
out those that would most impress the audience. Phi Beta
Kappa in college? Winner of a Silver Star in Vietnam?
Author of a book? Former president of the Chamber of
Commerce? Elected to YPO (Young Presidents Organiza-
tion)?

Open this way: "Ladies and gentlemen, I could talk
long about our speaker's accomplishments: that he was a
magna cum laude at Penn State, that he was elected "Man
of the Year" by the Chamber of Commerce in 1988, that
he was the youngest president in his company's history. . . ."

But I'd Rather Say

You've only skimmed off the cream of his accomplishments, but you sound as if you could have gone on five minutes more reciting equally impressive achievements.

Then you stop the listing by saying, "But I'd rather talk about an experience the speaker had when he was . . ."

Then pick a personal experience you had with the speaker. *One who's a leader knows his speaker personally, or, if not personally, then something personal about him.*

Have you played golf with him? Did you serve on a committee with her? Do you go to the same church?

From that experience pick out an anecdote that shows the character of the man: his concern for others, his "cool" in a crisis, his sense of vision.

I once introduced a federal judge this way: "I could tell you that our speaker once served as secretary of welfare in Harrisburg, or that he was chancellor of the Philadelphia Bar Association, or that he's a published biblical scholar, but I'd rather talk about the time I ran into him briefly at the train station. He asked me about my wife. I told the judge she was in the hospital recovering from a small operation, and the next day yellow roses—my wife's favorite—arrived at her hospital bed."

And then I added, "Now what does that say about our speaker? Not only that he's blessed with the gifts of administration as well as compassion. A busy man but not too busy for the thoughtful, kind gesture. Some people talk concern but don't carry it out. Our speaker doesn't just offer an expression of feeling; he's the executive who puts that feeling into deed.

"I give to you a man who is not only an efficient administrator of justice but a benevolent and kind man."

Once I had to introduce an insurance executive whom I didn't know personally. I called his secretary and asked her to repeat to me a story he often tells on himself or some human-interest story about him that wouldn't appear in the résumé. (Secretaries—if pressed—always seem to come up with some story about the boss that is funny yet flattering.)

This time the secretary was new on the job, so I had to dig deeper. "The résumé mentions his coaching Little League. Does he still do it?"

"Yes," she replied.

"Has his team been winning?"

"Oh, Mr. Humes, don't mention that! I'm afraid the word is that he hasn't yet had a winning season!"

That was all I needed. In my introduction I rattled off some of his startling achievements, and then I said: "But I'd rather say that our speaker is a *loser* [pause]. As a coach for his Little League team outside Hartford, he hasn't a winning season yet.

"But what does that say about our speaker? Here is the president of a top insurance company who has the time to coach kids. If a great leader is one measured by his worth to society, our speaker is tops. Our speaker is one whom men look up to—and so do boys! Maybe a loser in baseball but a winner everywhere else."

A Good Presentation
Is a Portrait

To fashion an introduction, find a story about the speaker. Let the audience see him so they can identify with him at home.

It is all right to mention the milestones in the speaker's life, but don't forget the man who made them! That's like painting a portrait with only a background, not a body. A good presentation is a miniportrait.

GOING FOR THE GREEN

· · · · · · · · · ·

Leaders make money or make others give money. Today the easiest way to raise yourself to the leadership level is to raise money.

Is it hard to raise money? Yes, if you're asking for gifts of a hundred dollars. But getting a gift of a thousand or even a hundred thousand dollars is far easier.

Why? Because the fat cats are easier to find and used to giving.

So volunteer to be a fund raiser. No one else wants the job, and it's the quickest way to meet and get to know the movers and shakers of your community. All you have to know is the language of soliciting. I call them the Four D's for Donors: defiance, design, donation, and duel.

Defiance

Your committee or staff will give you a list of names of contacts. Use your staff, which will do everything for you: list the would-be donors, write letters, and even arrange for appointments. Staff members will do everything but solicit. That they run away from, yet it's so simple.

The first step is psychological.

You must psych yourself into believing that you are doing this captain of industry a favor. You are giving him the chance to ennoble his purpose in life; you are widening the dimensions of his leadership.

Don't think you're like a teenager again asking your dad for a new car, a bigger allowance, or a college vacation in Florida. You're going in as an equal—seller to buyer. You are selling him the opportunity to bring more meaning into his life. *In a sense, you're selling him a ticket to heaven.*

So don't crawl in on bended knee. Stride in with a purposeful gait, look him right in the eyes, and say, "Mr. Bigwig, I'd like to take a moment of your time and talk about the new gymnasium."

GOING FOR THE GREEN

Design

What do you say to Mr. Bigwig? For your presentation, paint a picture of that new gymnasium, the new library, the community swimming pool.

A would-be donor isn't going to give to something abstract like the Humes Fund or Churchill Foundation. But he might endow a university chair in public speaking or a Churchill chair in World War II history. The donor likes to visualize what he's giving to.

If you have an artist's conception of the swimming pool or gymnasium, so much the better. But don't let the picture do your talking.

You must keep practicing your presentation until you are excited about it. Remember what Churchill said: "There is in that act of preparing the moment you start caring." If your donor-to-be sees you really care about the project, he'll listen.

Tell him about the gymnasium's new facilities for women. Show him how the swimming pool will be in easy reach of ghetto youngsters.

There is only one statistic the would-be-donor has to know, and that is how much it costs. Don't reel off a whole round of statistics—save them for when they're better heard—as answers to his questions later. You don't want to numb him with numbers.

Just pick one or two startling facts, such as that only 6 percent of high school graduates knew who were the losers in World War II or that swimmers in nearby rivers and streams run a 60 percent risk of being contaminated.

Put passion in your presentation. Put some romance in your recital. Appeal to his sense of history or humanity. Describe how he can build bodies, expand minds, save lives.

Make your pitch short, but not short in feeling.

Donation

If the would-be-donor needs to have a *specific picture* in mind before he gives, the solicitor has to have a *specific figure* in mind before he asks.

You yourself don't have to figure out the amount you should ask. It's better if you don't. Let your staff arrive at a figure. They can find out his general worth, his annual income, and his history of previous gifts to other groups.

When you've finished your pitch, make your request. "Mr. Bigwig, we were hoping you would make a gift of five thousand."

Even better: "We are choosing fifty captains for our million-dollar library drive. And each captain is a giver of twenty thousand dollars."

Duel

When you solicit, your "prime time" is not when you begin talking but when you end. It is that moment just *after* you have asked him for that fifty thousand dollars.

GOING FOR THE GREEN

That is "high noon" at the O.K. Corral, and you must let him draw first. Wait until he answers before you say anything. The wait—not the asking—is the hardest part, but it's the easy formula for gift giving.

If you speak first after the request, you've lost him perhaps forever. When you say something like "We hope you will consider it" or "I'll call you back next week," you've stepped down from being an equal. You're back to being a teenager asking Dad for the car. Wait, he may need time to figure out his cash-flow situation.

Wait, wait, wait—until his eyes blink. While waiting, imagine yourself as a statue—without a flicker of movement.

If he answers first, he almost never says no. He might say, "Could I give twenty-five thousand this year and twenty-five thousand the next?" Or "Could Dick Smith and I be cocaptains at twenty-five thousand each?" Or even "Could I get back to you next week?"

On that rare occasion he does say no, at least you've taken his measure as an equal and you've won his respect. He will remember you and regard you as a future leader.

By the way, if he does say he will call back in a week, wait ten days or two weeks and then call him at lunchtime—when he's *not* there!

He might not have even thought of your visit and request—many of us postpone a decision by putting it out of our minds—so don't catch him unawares by a phone call. If he's asked for a sudden decision, it might be a sad one for you.

But by a phone message, you are gently reminding him.

THE SIR WINSTON METHOD

He'll call back; the top executives all do. And I'll bet your answer will be a good one.

To raise money, you don't have to be rich. The technique is more psychological than financial. You have to go in as an equal, then wait for his answer, so you go out as an equal.

The language of leadership is more than just words; it is poise and presence.

A Prop, Not
A Crutch

. . . .

No Leader
Hides Behind Slides

Slides are sometimes necessary—to display a sketch, promote a design, explain statistics. Fine. *Use them. But don't overuse and abuse them.*

For too many executives, slides are a substitute for speaking. They don't have to deliver a talk; they just have to "introduce" each slide.

Boring! Think back to when friends invited you over for dinner to watch their slides from their recent trip to Europe: "And here's the Arc de Triomphe [slash of the slide]. And the Louvre [slash of the slide]. And here's Helen and me in front of you know what [slash of a slide of the Eiffel Tower]."

Yet executives do much the same thing when they deliver a presentation that is a series of comments sandwiched in between slides.

Slides Are Not the Language of Leadership

Slides are like drugs. There is a danger of becoming overdependent.

I wrote earlier, "A speech should be the oral projection of your personality, experiences, and ideas." I said "oral projection," not "mechanical projection." No inanimate screen can match a flesh-and-blood presentation.

This is a leadership book—not some technical manual—and you, the speaker, have to decide whether you want to be a leader or a technician.

If you want to resign yourself to a technician's role, keep on introducing a series of slides. But if you aim to be a leader, let slides be a prop, not a crutch.

When I press corporate executives on why they fill up their presentations with slides, they give two reasons. First, they say, "Well, you know the saying 'A picture is worth a thousand words.' " Then they add, "You ought to see the terrific job our graphics department does in working up our visual aids."

The two reasons mask the real reason:

Little Boys Like Toys

CEOs are fond of their perks. One of these is access to the best state-of-the-art projectors and slide equipment. It is like their limos and private washrooms. They like commanding a visual display to be worked up at the snap of a finger. And just because it's there to use, they overuse it.

Americans, particularly those in the business world, have a naive faith in anything mechanical. They are suckers for any new gadget or contraption that they think will do their work for them.

And that's the real reason why they become dependent on slides. It is an escape from the stark challenge of facing an audience. They turn over the responsibility to a machine. Now in answer to the Chinese adage "One picture [may be] worth a thousand words." I like another Chinese maxim: "The tongue can paint what the eye can't see."

When a speaker subordinates himself to the slide projector and makes his talk little more than captions for a disjointed series of pictures, he is stepping down from the role of leader. The speaker who lets a machine make his points for him only debases his own authority; he becomes a technician. As he diminishes his qualifications, he demolishes his chance to become a leader.

Slides Are Appetizers,
Not the Entrée

Does that mean you should never use slides? Of course not. A slide makes a great appetizer or dessert—but not the whole meal. A slide is a piece of stage business, and when used to explain abstract data like statistics or reorganization procedures, it not only is helpful but offers a refreshing change of pace.

A Handkerchief
Out of a Hat, Not a
Security Blanket

Visual aids should reinforce the speech, not replace it. The display shouldn't deflect attention from the speaker, nor should it detract from the message.

One head of a utilities conglomerate chose this way to present his slides. He posted his chart comparing tonnage on trucking, rail, and shipping lines at the rear of the room. Toward the end of the speech he strode off the podium to the back of the room. People turned expectantly around and fixed their eyes on the clearly marked chart in red, green, and black. The speaker had exploited the audience's focusing on the chart as a good wrapup for his talk. For him the visual aid was not a security blanket but a handkerchief pulled out of the hat like a magician. That's how slides can become the language of leadership.

A PROP, NOT A CRUTCH

An easy acronym sums up my do's and don'ts about SLIDES:

Slogan: Make the caption under each slide a *slogan*, a punch phrase, or a one-sentence line. Don't write an epistle.

Large: Put the print of the slogan in *large* caps.

Illustration: Keep the *illustration*, picture, or graph simple and uncluttered.

Directional: Don't use a *directional* stick or pointer. It's too distracting.

Erase: *Erase* one picture before you move to the next one. Otherwise it detracts from your talk. If there is a series of slides, have black ones in between.

Speech: Don't read your *speech* from a series of slide captions. Your audience can read. You are delivering a speech, not a series of introductions to slides.

A Speaker Is Not an Engineer but an Executive

In fact, he is a *leader*—at least for the time he presides at the podium. Don't demote yourself to a technician. Don't be dependent on slides. They become a crutch, and you become professionally a cripple—a lame excuse for a leader. The language of leadership is not reading off slides!

But if you use your slides as props, you elevate not only yourself but the audience's understanding of your message.

E i g h t e e n

AT WITS'

END

· · · · · · · · · ·

What Entertains Endures

What is the end objective to speech humor? Get laughs? Relax the audience? No. The real purpose is to put across a point in an entertaining way. What entertains endures—longer.

Advertisers know that. That's why the winning commercials each year are funny. But the real purpose of those TV ads is to make sales, not laughs.

THE SIR WINSTON METHOD

I tell that to clients who're about to make talks. Actually I almost have to yell it to them: Real leaders don't begin with a joke! A lot of times I run into a deaf ear—because at every dinner meeting the speaker opens with a joke; that doesn't make it right. Most speakers speak ten minutes too long; that doesn't make it right. Most speakers you see are twenty pounds overweight; that doesn't make it right.

Today more and more people skip the rich desserts. More and more choose chablis instead of martinis. But they cannot resist the instant gratification of the opening joke.

Why? Because a speech without laughs offers no tangible gratification until the applause at the end—even if the applause is often perfunctory. Well, the speaker should realize that the laughter following most opening jokes is just as perfunctory.

I don't like jokes in speeches. I do like wit and humor. What is the difference? Well, a joke is to humor what pornography is to erotic language in a good novel.

A joke that is told just to get a laugh reminds me of the Parisian street vendor who peddles pornographic postcards saying, "You vant a feelthy picture?" On the other hand, a love scene in a novel caps a blossoming romance between the hero and heroine.

In short, the opening joke is tacked onto the speech. But the light anecdote that is woven into your talk is humor.

The trick is to turn the joke into an anecdote.

A Tacked-on
Joke Is Tacky

The first rule is: Don't begin with a joke. A joke before you begin your talk is a tacked-on joke. It is tacked onto the speech that follows. A tacked-on joke is "tacky."

So don't open with a joke. As I wrote earlier, the beginning of your talk is the time to emblazon your theme and dramatize the current problem. If chuckles are what you're looking for, remember that the same joke, if made into an anecdote, will get more laughter in the middle of your talk—when a joke isn't expected.

Jokes, No;
Anecdotes, Yes

What is the difference between a joke and anecdote? It is the difference between fiction and fact. An anecdote is supposed to be true—even if many are apocryphal (an anecdote doesn't have to be authentic to be told). The subject of an anecdote is famous or at least real, and what that subject did has to be believable. "Jesus on the golf course" or "the pope in a whorehouse" fails to meet the test.

Because I do a good imitation of Churchill, I weave a lot of Churchill stories into my talks.

Almost every speech touches on change—the need to adopt new policies or to stick to old ones. If it's the former,

THE SIR WINSTON METHOD

I relate Churchill's famous encounter with the two-hundred-pound Bessie Braddock in 1955. Bessie in her fishmonger voice said to Churchill, "Winston, you are drunk." And Churchill replied, "Bessie, you are ugly, but tomorrow I shall be sober."

Unfortunately, since I first popularized the anecdote in the 1960's, it has become a little too well known. But because Mrs. Braddock told the story to me and because I have played Churchill onstage, I still find the story useful to emphasize the need for change.

For the need not to change, I recount this Churchill anecdote:

At a receiving line at the White House at a state dinner, a belle whose figure would make an hourglass envious was introduced to Winston Churchill. The British statesman caught the name of Lee as well as the honeyed tones that suggested southern lineage. "Are you related to the general?" Churchill asked.

"Indeed, Mr. Churchill," she answered. "My family is proud of its connection to Master Robert, and we bitterly opposed the Reconstruction imposed by the North."

"Madam," Churchill replied, "so would have I. In your case 'reconstruction' would be blasphemous."

That story about Churchill reminds me of another anecdote about another world statesman whom I have also played onstage, Benjamin Franklin. For business talks that often touch on bulging costs and slim budgets I tell this tale:

AT WITS' END

At a reception at Versailles given by King Louis XVI in 1777 for Benjamin Franklin, scores of young beautiful women vied for the attention of the aged American minister to France. After one scrawny young lady had engaged Franklin's attention, the king commented: "Unfortunately the mademoiselle doesn't do justice to her décolletage. God did not endow her."

Franklin, who was urging French assistance to the colonial cause, replied: "Yes, sire, God did not endow her, but you can endow us. For my country's treasury has the same problem as that young lady—an uncovered deficit."

For high costs that promise too little return you might want to weave into your talk this shopping expedition by Zsa Zsa Gabor:

The ageless Hollywood actress stepped into Giorgio's on Rodeo Drive. In the men's department black-polka-dotted pink pajamas caught her eye. She asked the salesman, "How much are they?"

"Miss Gabor," answered the man at the counter, "these Dior-designed men's sleepwear are five hundred dollars."

"Darlink," she replied, "for that price the pajamas should come with a man in them."

Are rising costs or declining sales the main headache? Which problem takes priority? For the mention of "priority"—a concept for many talks—I slip into the talk this baseball tale:

A couple of Augusts ago Sparky Anderson's Detroit Tigers hit a slump when their bats were cold as January. Sparky called his director of minor-league scouting.

"Sparky," answered the scout "you ought to see this left-hander. He's a phenom. Why, the other day when he pitched, they couldn't get a hit off him. The only guy who got wood to the ball was one guy who hit two long fouls."

"Forget the pitcher," said Sparky. "Sign up the guy who hit the foul ball."

The Anecdote Advantage

Jokes can bomb. Anecdotes don't. The fellow who tries to foist "a funny" as his opener can fall on his face. But the anecdote has a parachute.

Unlike "the horse in the bar" or "duck in the store," it is real and relevant.

With a joke a laugh is a must. But with an anecdote, it is a bonus. It pushes a point by entertaining. The anecdote is like a candy-coated vitamin pill. It not only gives zest to a point but tastes good going down.

An Anecdote Is a
Page from *People* Magazine

Time magazine has for many years devoted a page to items about celebrities. Over the years the feature proved so popular that *People* magazine was formed to expand on those celebrity items. Some call anecdotes about celebrities gossip. Well, gossip sells, and it can sell your point, too.

Anecdotes Lighten and Enlighten

Anecdotes make a speech come alive. They pep up what might be a ponderous speech. They lighten a talk while enlightening a point.

If you can't find the right story about a star, tell a funny happening about number one: yourself.

Think of the craziest situation you once found yourself in. Maybe it was a strange mixup of names or a weird misunderstanding.

What would you fill in under the *Reader's Digest* heading "Life's Most Embarrassing Moment"?

Every Anecdote Has an Adage

In each of life's funny experiences there's a lesson to be learned. Think through that crazy or comic situation that happened to you. If you had known more, listened better, or seen more clearly, would things have gone differently? That can translate in a speech to poor research, poor communication or poor planning.

THE SIR WINSTON METHOD

I tell this story about poor research:

In 1956 as a Young Republican I was an usher for a GOP thousand-dollar-a-plate dinner that President Eisenhower attended. The gala was held in a huge downtown arena. Just before Eisenhower's appearance, a Secret Service agent spotted my official badge and said, "Where's the men's room? The President needs to find it."

I was caught unawares. I didn't know whether the men's room was the room fifty yards around the left or the room fifty yards to the right.

But I pointed to the right, saying, "Down that way, sir," and I began running in that direction to make sure I was right. When I got there, I found I had chosen wrong. Seeing in the distance the President and an aide turning the corner, coming toward me, I opened the door and shouted, "Everybody out, everybody out. Emergency. The President of the United States!"

Some distressed lady was flushed out like a startled grouse. I turned the door back against the side wall—to hide the telltale sign.

With my hand at salute, the President entered, and I closed the door. The President must have noticed the presence of some uncustomary dispensaries, for when he emerged, his blue eyes looked at me, drilled two laser holes, and muttered, "Poor staff work."

AT WITS' END

Joke into Anecdote

One day a student said to me, "Professor Humes, your lecture—so much to listen to—all your stories! We haven't led such an interesting life, so tell us where do you find some of your anecdotes about Churchill and Franklin?"

Well, I told them that I've read lots of biographies and take notes. I also confessed that I take some shortcuts. I tell some "jokes" in the middle of the talk *as if they were true and really happened.*

Business has been pretty bad lately. But it could be worse. It could be as bad as the men's store I went into the other day in Philadelphia.

When I asked the owner how he was, he answered, "Terrible, terrible. Monday we had only one customer. Tuesday we had none at all. And then Wednesday was worse than Tuesday."

I said, "How could Wednesday be worse than Tuesday when you had no customers?"

"Oh it was worse. The man who bought a suit on Monday came in and wanted a refund."

Now that didn't actually happen to me, but I told it as if it had. In doing so, I turned a joke into an anecdote.

For the problem of undercapitalization, I've recounted this incident:

No matter how strong our intentions are or how great our ideas, we still have to possess the necessary resources. I remember when I, as a student, visited a

THE SIR WINSTON METHOD

friend in the South, my roommate and I had tickets to a testimonial dinner for a town's leading citizen. He was president of the bank; the big office building bore his name. The successful businessman was called upon to tell the story of his life.

"Friends and neighbors," he said in a husky voice, "when I first came in here some thirty years ago, I walked to your town on a muddy road. I had only one suit on my back, one pair of shoes on my feet, and all my earthly possessions were wrapped in a red bandanna tied to a stick I carried on my shoulder.

"This city has been good to me. Today I'm chairman of the board of the bank. I own a hotel, apartment buildings, and office buildings. I own three companies in twenty-one cities. I serve on the boards of many clubs. Yes, my friends, this town has been good to me."

When he finished, a young man near me asked a question. "Sir, could you tell me what you had wrapped in that red bandanna when you walked into the town some thirty years ago?"

"I think, son," he said, "I was carrying about a hundred thousand in traveler's checks and two hundred thousand in government bonds."

The truth is I didn't witness that. I read it. But telling it as an anecdote, I can weave the story into a talk.

By telling it as if it really happened, I put an "anecdote" mask upon a joke. It works as long as the tale is believable and tells a point.

AT WITS' END

If I have distorted fact, remember there is humor license as well as poetic license.

At fund raisers I often regale audiences with this "anecdote":

Back in my hometown in upstate Pennsylvania this poor little tailor and his wife struggled to give his three sons college educations. Through his sacrifice one became an accountant, one a lawyer, and the third a doctor.

On his sixtieth birthday he said to the boys, "You know, Mama and I never have taken a trip since we left the old country. Could you see fit to give us the tickets to go back to Europe?"

The accountant answered, "Well, Dad, I'd like to, but you know we just put in a new kitchen."

So he turned to the lawyer, who replied, "I'm sorry, Dad, but it's a bad time. We just bought that new Chris Craft for the lake."

Then he looked at the doctor, but he replied, "Dad, I'm sorry, but you know, we just bought that new condominium in Miami."

"Boys," he said sorrowfully, "I never told you this before, but we had so little money, Mama and I, when we started out that we didn't even have money for a marriage license."

"But, Dad," one of the sons said, "you know what that makes us—"

"Yes," he replied, "and *cheap* ones, too."

Now even if the audience realizes that it probably didn't happen, it doesn't matter. I've "anecdotized" a joke into a good story about money giving.

The Three R's

The three R's about making a joke into an anecdote are these: It must be *realistic,* it must be *relevant,* and it should be *retellable.*

If it is *realistic* or believable, it can be easily woven into the warp and woof of your talk. Then it has to be *relevant,* to relate to a point you want to stress. And finally it must be *retellable* or in good taste. Crudity is not part of the language of leadership. Nor are ethnic or religious slurs.

THE KING
AND YOU

· · · · · · · · · ·

"Rose Garden Rubbish"

Tom Brokaw said to me in 1977, "Now you have to admit you didn't generally write the really heavy, tough speeches. You wrote a lot of what's called the Rose Garden rubbish."

Peter Benchley, before he wrote *Jaws,* was a speech writer for LBJ, and that's the name he gave to all the ceremonial talks the President gives in the White House Rose Garden when he salutes the Easter Seal girl or greets a visiting prince.

Brokaw had it right about me. But, then, what most of us White House speech writers wrote were ceremonials: a toast to a prime minister, a eulogy for Eisenhower, the inscription on a presidential medal for Duke Ellington, a plaque to be placed on the moon when the astronauts landed in 1969. All this was the work of White House speech writers.

Like the British queen, the President is the chief of state. He must preside at state dinners and ceremonial events, and on those occasions he must embody and articulate our nation's ideals and aspirations. He can't diminish the occasion by winging it. Just mouthing, "You're doing a great job," would be a verbal brushoff.

But the President doesn't have the time to study up on the visiting sultan or top Boy Scout, so the White House writers—like some anonymous functionary in Buckingham Palace—craft remarks.

The Greatest
Speeches Are Ceremonials

I didn't feel slighted by being asked to write these remarks for the President. The greatest speeches in history were ceremonial talks: the Gettysburg Address and Pericles' Funeral Oration.

Some of Ronald Reagan's best-known addresses were

ceremonial. Think of his words when the astronauts crashed in 1987 or his speech in Normandy in 1984, honoring the fortieth anniversary of D-day.

I liked to pull the heartstrings. In fact, some of the White House staff called me "the Schmaltz King." I took pride in the title. But to be honest, as a writer I wasn't in the same league with a Peggy Noonan or a Ken Khachigian, two of Reagan's top writers.

But I worked hard on the "Rose Garden rubbish." What spurred me was that the writer was always invited to the ceremonial occasion. The look on the visiting delegation's faces was reward enough for finding the right line, that bit of verse, or the historical anecdote that would fill hearts with pride.

Queen for a Day

What some CEOs don't understand is that when they preside at a company occasion giving a watch to a retiring employee or a plaque to an achiever, they play the role of king. They are the kings of their companies or corporations. They are for that moment Kings or Queens for the Day.

But many just wing it by mouthing trite pleasantries. The result is they diminish not only the men they honor but their own stature.

When You Prepare
a Little, You Care a Lot

If they would prepare a little, their listeners would know they care a lot about the people who make up their companies.

All of you, at one time or another, have had to salute a departing colleague or award a plaque or certificate. So you're not the CEO! At least you're his deputy for the occasion, as Prince Charles is on behalf of the queen of England. If you are not king for the day, you're a prince.

So don't just mouth the ordinary platitudes without preparing. You'll dull what might have been a majestic moment in the recipient's life.

When You Just Go
Through the Motions, You Don't
Stir the Emotions

Short ceremonial talks will be remembered long after a speech on a bond referendum or a talk on Thailand. Why? Events are better etched in our mind than words— particularly emotional events. Robert Kennedy's most remembered talk is the eulogy of his brother.

Speaking of the death of Kennedy, I delivered a eulogy to the Pennsylvania House of Representatives at the same time, and each year it is read aloud in the Pennsylvania Assembly. Edward Moore, the eighty-year-old parliamentarian at the time, said it was the finest talk he had ever heard in fifty years of service.

Why did my talk so stir the emotions? Because it was an emotional occasion!

But eulogies aren't the only ceremonials that bring listeners close to tears.

A few well-crafted words about the humanity or heroism of an honoree can tap tears—whether it is a reception for a retiree or an award for some achiever.

For such a talk, the leader doesn't just go through the motions. He tries to stir the emotions of pride, love, and respect. *The good speaker sees such an occasion as an opportunity for leadership.*

That doesn't mean you have to write out a long talk. Brief is better! Anyway, you don't want to be seen reading such a speech. The leader should look as if he were talking from his heart.

In the Kingdom of the Blind, the One-Eyed Man Is King

In fact, all you have to do is just take the time to reflect a bit before the occasion. When you prepare, it shows that you care. Caring is a criterion for leadership. We look up to those who recognize our contributions, express our hopes, and care for our feelings.

Just three minutes of preparation can make your words

remembered for the rest of the honoree's life. If you do that, you'll be doing more than most. The typical person just wings it by looking at a bio or reading off a plaque. Remember, in the kingdom of the blind the one-eyed man is king.

The Three M's

My three-minute workout is called the three M's: *memory, message, mission.*

Fix your *memory* on just one happening in the honoree's life that tells the kind of gentleman or lady he or she is.

It could be a story familiar to many. Better yet, it is something only you know about: the advice he gave you in your first days with the company, his kindness to you and your family when your wife was sick, even a funny gift he surprised you with on your birthday.

Flesh out the story. Re-create your conversation. Paint a picture of where it took place.

Then mine the *message* in that memory. Does the story reveal his innate decency, his thoughtfulness to others, his sense of humor—particularly about himself?

Inspiration
for Our Aspiration

And finally the *mission*. In the light of his or her example what should the rest of us be doing? How can we better serve our companies, our communities, and our fellow men! In other words, what is our *mission?*

His ideals are a lesson. His example is inspiration for our aspiration.

Think of the Gettysburg Address. The timelessness of Lincoln's two-minute talk is proof that the simple three M's formula of memory, message, and mission works.

Time Tactic

Some of my students and business clients complain that they couldn't come up with the right personal story or anecdote in three days, much less three minutes. For one thing, they hardly know the people they're honoring.

One substitute for such a story is the "time tactic." Pick a year—the year the person being honored was born, the year he came to the company—or if you're dedicating a wing or a new office, pick the year the original company was founded or the building was erected.

Then reach for the almanac and take note of who famous was born that year. What were the big movies, the best sellers, and the hit songs when he or she was born or first came to the company?

To honor the sixtieth birthday of a judge born in 1926, I looked in the almanac and found that Queen Elizabeth was born the same year. I fashioned a talk about two babies who were born to rule and preside.

When I check out the movies or best sellers of a particular year, I never fail to find at least one title of a song, movie, or book that is an apt description of the person to be honored. For a shipping executive, I discovered he was born in 1954, the year of *On the Waterfront* with Marlon Brando. Once I had to write a retirement talk for a Mellon Bank executive who had come to work for the Pittsburgh-based company in 1952, when a top song started "On a corner in a pawnshop in Pittsburgh, Pennsylvania."

Trivia Is Nostalgia

Does the time tactic sound as if you were preparing for a trivia contest? So what! Trivia is a turn-on—because it triggers fond memories. Mention a song or a movie, and you instantly think of whom you saw it with or whom you were dating. Trivia doesn't trivialize an event; it glamorizes it. It can associate the recipient with the aura of an author or actor. It gives a niche in history to the honoree. The audience might learn that the honoree's first day at the job was in 1963, when Kennedy was shot or the Beatles first went on the Ed Sullivan show.

Or they might learn that she was born in 1956, when the Soviets crushed the Hungarian uprising and Yankee pitcher Don Larsen pitched a perfect game in the World Series.

If you use the time tactic, you give meaning to a milestone. Don't just dab at details; paint the picture. Did he wear a crew cut in 1963? Did she wear a beehive? Who were the company's biggest clients then? Where was headquarters then located?

THE KING AND YOU

If you are dedicating a wing in a hospital, you can pick the year the original building was erected. And you can talk about the anesthetic and operating procedures then.

For such a ceremony of dedicating a hospital wing or hanging a portrait of a former company head, a personal story from the life of a doctor or the company president is best. The "time tactic" is at best a substitute for a personal vignette, but it does add a personal touch to what might be a mechanical presentation. You add warmth to what might be a cold formality.

And when you take the time to prepare by looking into the honoree's life or background, you care. And caring is the language of leadership.

READ A
SPEECH LIKE
REAGAN

....

Ronald Reagan was the "Great Communicator," right? Actually, Reagan was fired from his first communications job.

When he was graduated from Eureka College in Illinois, his first job was at a radio station. No doubt, his resonant baritone as well as his college acting experience helped land him the job.

Then why did the station fire him? Because he couldn't read the commercials convincingly. In other words, he was a flop at reading radio scripts.

The failure puzzled Reagan. He had a relaxed conversational patter that was popular with listeners. But the station's advertisers didn't like the way he read their commercials. He was flat.

While out of work, Reagan asked himself what he had done wrong. How could he bring credibility to his reading of a script? He tried listening to radio transcriptions of his hero President Franklin Roosevelt, who, he knew, read his speeches. What was FDR's secret?

Through practice Reagan discovered that if he didn't look at the script while reciting the lines, he could simulate the pace of conversational delivery. After all, he had learned in his college drama experience that he could memorize lines easily. So he worked out a technique of looking at a line or two and then looking away from it to "conversationalize" into the microphone the phrase or two that he had just memorized.

The technique wasn't new to Reagan. He had developed it while auditioning for roles in school plays. Others might have read from the playscript while trying out for a part, but Reagan would memorize the line and then look at the play director while reciting the line.

When the commentator who had replaced Reagan took a job at another station, Reagan asked for a second chance. This time he looked down to memorize a line or two of the commercial, then covered it with his hands, looked up, and "conversationalized" it into the microphone. The new technique made Reagan a hit with the station advertisers.

Reagan had discovered the secret of reading a speech like a Franklin Roosevelt or a Winston Churchill.

The Greatest Speakers Read Their Speeches

In speaking there are three axioms: *Bad speakers* read speeches. *Good speakers* read from notes. *Great speakers* read speeches!

Franklin Roosevelt, Winston Churchill, Douglas MacArthur all read their speeches. Memorable phrases like FDR's "The only thing we have to fear is fear itself" didn't spring from the top of his head. Kennedy's *"Ich bin ein Berliner"* was not extemporaneous.

Churchill, MacArthur, and Lincoln painfully wrote out their speeches and polished them to perfection. Ted Sorensen for John Kennedy and Peggy Noonan for Ronald Reagan toiled long and hard in their White House offices honing a phrase and shaping a sentence for a presidential address. The language of leadership does not leap out of nowhere.

In my opening class at the University of Pennsylvania, I ask for volunteers to stand up at the lectern and read an editorial from *The Wall Street Journal* or *The New York Times*.

I tell them, "Read it as if you were a speaker at a dinner." The student volunteer then tries to read the talk with some verve and style, yet no matter how hard he or she tries, the effort fails. Why? Two big reasons: (1) Their pacing or delivery sounds unnatural or "unconversational" and (2) they lose their eye contact with the audience.

The Reagan formula cures both problems. I call his formula the snapshot/snatch plan.

For practice take out your morning paper. Pick one editorial or an op-ed column. Set a makeshift lectern of a box or a drawer on top of a table, and place the article on the box or bottom of the drawer as you would a speech to be read.

Look down and "snapshot" or "eye-photograph" a phrase, or "snatch," of words. (I call it a snatch because that's what Churchill called any oral chunk of words—easy to utter in one breath.) Bring your head back up, and then, while looking at the lamp at the far end of the room as if it were a listener, "conversationalize" what you just memorized. Pause, and then look down again and snapshot the next phrase or snatch. Bring your head back up and repeat.

Thou Shalt Never
Speak When Thine Eyes Are
Looking Down!

There is only one rule you have to follow: *Never, never, never let words come out of your mouth when your eyes are looking down.*

Now have you tried out this snapshot/snatch plan? If you have, you'll be saying to yourself, as one of my students once told me, "Mr. Humes, these pauses, while I bring up my head to speak and then while I lower my eyes to memorize the next couple of lines are awkward. It makes my delivery jerky, and anyway, that pause is going to lose my audience. Their minds are going to turn to something else."

Wrong! That pause does allow you to read a speech in snatches while keeping your eyes fixed upon your audience. But even more important, that pause allows your listeners to digest your words.

If you've ever run out of gas and then poured gas from a can into the tank, you'll remember how if you pour it too fast, the narrow tube rejects it and triggers a back flow or an overflow.

In the same way a listener rejects a speech that's read. Without a pause, the ear turns off.

Listen to any conversation. You don't chatter nonstop. You take pauses. Pauses are what make a speech sound conversational. Listen to tapes of Roosevelt, Churchill, MacArthur, Martin Luther King, and Everett Dirksen; their delivery is not nonstop. They pause. The effect is deliberative, statesmanlike.

The Pause Is Powerful

In fact, any teacher of speech will tell you that the pause is the most powerful tool in the speaker's arsenal.

So let's try the exercise of reading that article again: Look down. *Snapshot a snatch*. Bring your head up, and *pause* for a second. Conversationalize your snatch of words.

Why do I ask you to pause after you bring your head up? Because most speakers start to speak while their heads are still moving back up. By taking that extra pause, you fool the audience into thinking you're just glancing at notes and not actually reading the speech.

When I was a young boy, my family had a terrible car accident on an icy road. That moment before the crash seemed like an eternity, but it was hardly more than a couple of seconds.

In the same way the pause seems like an eternity to you, but to your audience it is a microsecond.

Let's try it again.

Look down. Snapshot a snatch. Look up—all the way up. *Pause.* Then "conversationalize" your snatch of words.

Now continue this snapshot/snatch plan for the rest of the editorial or article.

At first you may remember to bring your head back up and pause, but after some minutes of speaking you'll find yourself sliding back into starting to speak before your head is all the way back up.

Don't worry. Keep practicing. By the way, when I teach corporate executives this snapshot/snatch plan, who do you think picks up the technique the quickest? Lawyers? Engineers? Women? Intellectuals? Extroverts?

The answer is jocks—men or women who are good golf or tennis players. Basically it is not a mental but an eye-hand skill. Television anchors are not necessarily picked for their brains, but they're pros at reading texts.

That does not mean that you have to be an Olympian

medalist to read a speech. Actually it's easier than learning
to ride a bike. If you ever played golf or tennis, you'll
recall how a new grip the club pro taught you seemed so
strange at first but then became natural. The snapshot/
snatch plan of reading a speech is the same.

Let's do the exercise again:

1. Look down and snapshot a snatch.

2. Look up and *pause.*

3. Deliver the snatch and *pause.*

4. Look down and take another snapshot.

5. Look up and *pause.*

6. Deliver another snatch.

Remember, the pause is the major tool in reading a
speech. It not only helps you "eye-photograph" your text,
phrase by phrase, or snatch by snatch, but also lets the
audience digest your words better.

Try the technique out on an excerpt from Churchill's
iron curtain speech in 1946:

A shadow has fallen upon the scene
    [pause]
So lately lighted by the Allied victory
    [pause]
From Stettin in the Baltic to Trieste in the Adriatic
    [pause]
An iron curtain has descended across the continent.

Does the pause still sound labored, stilted? Does it still seem artificially jarring to you? Maybe it does to you, but to your audience you'll be sounding like Winston Churchill!

The pause that seems an eternity to you is only a microsecond that "punctuates" the sentence, builds audience anticipation, and helps listener understanding.

If you still don't believe me, look at yourself on videotape. The corporate executives I teach are always amazed when they see themselves on the screen. The pause that they thought so awkward makes their delivery sound more like their conversational style.

In our conversations we often pause to think of the right words, to organize our thoughts, to frame the next sentence.

When you read a speech without pauses, you seem to be reading a speech someone else wrote for you. When you pause, you sound sincere; you sound as if you're trying to come up with the right words to express your feelings.

The pause—whether you're reading a speech, speaking from notes, or speaking without notes—is the greatest tool in the language of leadership.

One more tip for reading a speech like a leader: Put it in leadership format.

In July 1990 I went to the dedication of the Nixon Library and Museum in California. There is displayed the original manuscript of his "Silent Majority" speech, which he delivered in October 1969.

Though his speech writers made contributions, the final result was mostly the work of Nixon himself, who wrote out the talk on yellow legal-size paper in the Lincoln Study. The final copy, which he used for his television address, is now exhibited on the wall of the replica of the Lincoln Study. The type-out of the speech does not resemble an article; it's a series of bullet lines—triple-spaced.

It reminded me of my visit to the Churchill Memorial at Fulton, Missouri, where I spoke in 1979. The manuscript for Churchill's iron curtain address is also on display there. The copy that Churchill read from the lectern in that college gymnasium looked much different from the one distributed to the press. Churchill's lectern copy looks like verse:

From Stettin in the Baltic
To Trieste in the Adriatic
An iron curtain has descended
Across the continent.

Print a Speech Like Prose, and It Comes Off Prosaically

Churchill believed a great speech was closer to poetry than to prose. After all, like poetry, it was written for the ear. To Churchill a speech was a form of poetry—unmetered, unrhymed verse. So he had it typed up that way.

Most speakers have their speeches typed to look like articles, and they read them like articles. They print them like prose, and they come off prosaically!

In an article, words succeed one another until the margin on the right side brings a halt—even if the line is mid-thought or mid-word. Then the words continue a line lower, and the processing of words continues rightward until the next margin. Lines do not stop at the end of a phrase or thought but at the end of a margin.

But for the language of leadership, lay it out like verse.

Reader-Friendly

At the University of Pennsylvania I require my graduate students to type out their speech presentations in the snatch by snatch form in triple space.

I make them indent every new sentence like a paragraph. All this makes the speech reader-friendly. Then I tell them, "Don't turn each page of the speech over as you finish reading it. It not only is distracting to the audience but lets them know you are reading your talk instead of speaking from notes. Fool them. Put your speech on the right side of the lectern, and then slide the finished page with your left hand to the left side of the lectern."

Man in the Arena

Some of my students say to me, "Professor Humes, is it all right if I don't read my speech? I do it better from notes."

"Fine," I tell them, "but you still have to hand in a

typed version of the speech in the triple-spaced verse format."

Actually I like it when they speak from notes—even better when they speak without any notes! That's the way I do it. That's the way former President Nixon does it. He gives speeches without notes—and even without a lectern in front of him. Nixon calls it "the man in the arena" format: To speak onstage bare of props—no lectern, no table, no chair.

It may look as if Nixon is speaking off the top of his head, but don't believe it! Hours of work went into his preparation. He wrote out the talk—word for word—and then committed it to memory.

Nixon has made a comeback from Watergate to become an elder statesman. How? By writing and speaking out. By not charging for his speeches, he can pick the most prestigious forums, and then he proceeds to overwhelm audiences by his masterly analysis of world affairs, spicing his talk with quotes from statesmen he has known and reinforcing his points with statistics on trade and literacy in third world nations—all without a note for ninety minutes. Pretty impressive for a man nearing eighty. Even his enemies have to respect his brilliance.

How does Nixon memorize it? The way Lincoln did. You've all heard the story of how Lincoln wrote the Gettysburg Address on the back of an envelope while riding a train.

Well, the fact is that Lincoln had already written out his speech days before he boarded the train. While riding to Gettysburg, Lincoln took an envelope from his pocket and

wrote on the back of it a series of key words: "Fourscore
. . . conceived . . . dedicated . . . a great war . . ."

It was a memory exercise he often used to prep himself
before speaking. At a banquet while others are eating their
dessert, I will often take the back of the dinner program
and do the same thing. I write a series of key words of
certain ideas or anecdotes as a memory exercise for the
speech I wrote long before. People may think I am writing
notes for my speech, but I don't use the notes when I
speak. It is my private mental workout.

At the University of Pennsylvania I demand that my
students write out their speeches even when they don't
read their speeches. Why? Speeches delivered from notes
ramble unless you have first organized your thoughts and
ideas into sentences on paper.

Many CEOs I talk to pride themselves that they speak
only from notes. I look at their notes:

1. History of company

2. New market trends

3. What's happening in Washington

4. New products

Fine, I say, but I make them first write out their
thoughts on each topic before. Then, when they speak
from notes, they don't ramble from topic to topic. They
speak like leaders because they have first organized their
thoughts and ideas into forceful sentences as leaders
should.

READ A SPEECH LIKE REAGAN

When they get up to speak, they don't have to remember exactly what they actually wrote out. It doesn't matter.

In fact, a speaker will be more conversational if he doesn't try to remember. Let the subconscious take over. Speak conversationally on each point. The time you spend working out your ideas and beliefs on paper will make you sound in command, clear and forceful—in the language of a leader.

In the spring of 1948 President Harry Truman read a speech on foreign affairs to the National Press Club. Because Truman never learned the Roosevelt or Reagan system of reading a speech, it got a listless response.

Afterward he answered questions. His crisp, salty replies got a standing ovation.

His White House aide Clark Clifford noted this. Against the opposition of the State Department, which always insists that Presidents—as well as secretaries of state and ambassadors—speak from preapproved and thoroughly vetted texts, Clifford suggested that Truman do away with prepared texts. Clifford, who read in the polls that Truman was twenty points behind Dewey, figured that they had nothing to lose.

Truman agreed. He hated reading speeches others had prepared for him. So Truman wrote out the talk himself and then reduced his talk to a series of bullet lines.

The first time he tried it out was for his Democratic National Convention acceptance speech in Philadelphia in 1948. On the train from Washington he went over his talk and jotted down key words. In Philadelphia he didn't get to speak until midnight because of opposition from southern Democrats, who later bolted the party. Still, Truman's speech electrified the weary delegates. It was the beginning of "Give 'em hell, Harry." His bullet technique pulled off the greatest upset in history. Harry Truman had discovered the language of leadership.

Twenty One

TALK YOUR
WAY TO THE
TOP

· · · · · · · · · ·

One speech made ex-actor Ronald Reagan the nominee for governor and a national leader in the Republican party.

One speech made William Jennings Bryan, a young unknown country lawyer from Nebraska, the leader of the Democratic party and nominee for President.

THE SIR WINSTON METHOD

One speech made Martin Luther King a world figure in the civil rights movement.

One speech by a lawyer named Russell Conwell built Temple University in Philadelphia.

One speech by Lee Iacocca saved Chrysler from bankruptcy.

What do all these speeches have in common? Why is Reagan's "Time for Choosing" in 1964 like William Jennings Bryan's "Cross of Gold" in 1896? Why is King's "I Have a Dream" speech on civil rights like Iacocca's speech on Chrysler?

Reagan's speech raised millions of dollars for Goldwater. Iacocca's speech won the congressional appropriation to save Chrysler from going out of business. King's speech recruited millions of volunteers worldwide for the civil rights movement. Conwell's "Acre of Diamonds" speech brought in millions of dollars to build a university.

Each of those addresses gives meaning to the phrase "language of leadership." Each of those speeches was a winner for the same reason. Each of those speeches had been tried out many times earlier before it won a national audience.

Ronald Reagan as a spokesman for General Electric spoke four times a day, four times a week. Before audiences in GE plants and Rotary Clubs he delivered his message about the evils of big government, wasteful bureaucracy, and runaway spending. By the time he addressed a national television audience on behalf of Goldwater he had honed his lines to perfection.

William Jennings Bryan tried out his "Cross of Gold"

speech on station crowds at railroad stops on the way to Chicago. Actually he had already shaped the talk in his earlier appearances to farm groups and Democratic party caucuses in Nebraska. At the Chicago convention his perfected lines electrified the delegates and won him the presidential nomination.

In sermons and speeches to civil rights groups Martin Luther King had already time-tested the lines that would make his "I Have a Dream" address in front of the Lincoln Memorial part of English literature.

Lee Iacocca and Russell Conwell gave their talks hundreds of times before they caught on—to make them the most sought-after speakers of their day.

I tell these facts to the CEO when I am asked by a top executive to draft a speech for the Boys Club of Newark.

I say to this CEO of a *Fortune* 500 company, "Look, Mr. Executive, I'll be happy to write a speech for this Boys Club dinner talk and then write another different talk when you speak a few months later to the United Fund of Chicago. And then perhaps I can draft another completely different talk—say, to a Chamber of Commerce or perhaps a college commencement audience. The more speeches I draft, the more money I make.

"But in the advertising for your company you push the same message. Why not do the same thing in a speech? Let me write one basic speech you can deliver with few changes to any audience. The only way to get a message across is to repeat it. And every time you deliver it you do it better. Every time you do it you learn what lines register and what anecdotes get a good response."

THE SIR WINSTON METHOD

I became a good speaker in 1965, after I had been defeated for reelection to the Pennsylvania Assembly in 1964. I volunteered for the American Bar Association to speak on the proposed constitutional amendment on presidential disability. I dramatized what might have happened if President John Kennedy, instead of being instantly killed in Dallas, had lived on for eighty days as President James Garfield had in 1881.

I gave my twenty-minute talk to Rotary Clubs, Grange groups, and League of Women Voter clubs across the state. After about the fifth time I gave the talk the speech was on automatic pilot. I no longer had to think what I was going to say next, it was automatic. As a result, I could concentrate on the audience.

Think back to the favorite story you tell your friends. You no longer have to think about it. The words come automatically and you instinctively learn all the techniques of speaking: when to pause and when to lower your voice to a whisper.

Richard Burton told me he learned more about acting every time he played *Hamlet*. Every time he played in the Old Vic, he came away knowing better how to set up key words or what gestures to make in reinforcing his words.

I had a chance to study Ronald Reagan on tapes before he became governor. He didn't patent that "Well" with the cock-of-his-head gesture until later in his career. The best gestures are not planned but come out instinctively once you have your talk down pat. Those gestures then become the "silent" language of leadership.

Half the grade I give each graduate student at the Uni-

Talk Your Way to the Top

versity of Pennsylvania is based on his or her final speech.
I make the student give it three times!

Each student has to get my okay on his or her topic. I
advise: "Think of a talk you can give the rest of your life,
one that is both fun and fact-filled, one that is not only
interesting but entertaining."

I draw on the blackboard two circles that overlap. One
I mark "Expertise," and the other I label "Audience Interest." And I tell my class that where the two overlap is
the subject they should speak on.

Many of my graduate students at the University of Pennsylvania are part-timers who hold full-time jobs. I told a
realtor to develop a speech on "The Ten Things to Look
For in Buying a House."

I advised a transportation safety executive in New Jersey
who mentioned to me his longtime interest in old ocean
liners to speak on the ten safety violations that sank the
Titanic.

A black student spoke on the boyhood of Martin Luther
King. He now finds himself in popular demand in churches
and service clubs and every January at the time of the King
holiday.

A Vietnam refugee entitled his talk "The Day I Became
an American Citizen." On days such as the Fourth of July
or Veterans Day in November, he is showered with invi-
tations.

Service clubs, by the way, try to find speakers way in
advance to fit the needs of the calendar: the Heart Fund or
Lincoln's Birthday in February, Library Week and Income
Tax Day in April, Law Day and Memorial Day in May,

and Father's Day and Flag Day in June. Almost every week of the year heralds some cause or honors some hero.

If you have some expertise on any of these topics, write your local clubs and volunteer your services. Don't be shy. Program chairmen are desperate to find speakers to fill the empty spaces on their club calendars.

Anytime you are invited to speak you become a leader—a leader in your community. By a series of talks in your city and nearby communities, you'll march to the head of your profession, be that accounting, law, or real estate.

A stockbroker I know has polished a fascinating account of the 1929 crash that is popular with Chambers of Commerce: "Why there Never Will Be a Black Monday as Black as November 1929."

Make Your Interests
Yield Dividends

Whatever your expertise, hobby, or interest make it pay dividends. Read up on it. Latch on to every sensational or humorous anecdote. Focus on famous people. What did they do on that eventful day? Did they panic or persist?

Write out your talk. Practice it. The best place I find to practice is the shower, where every voice becomes a resonant baritone in the echoing chamber. If you sing in the shower, why not orate? No one can hear you. In a hot shower your inhibitions melt and your emotions surge.

When you have worked out and practiced your talk, volunteer yourself—maybe at first to your church group or

PTA or the local high school. It is the first step on your
road to the top. And at every stop on the road you'll find
your words becoming more and more the language of leadership.

Practice Makes Perfection

Even more important, by delivering your one speech over
and over, you will discover instinctively the secrets of
speech delivery: the pause, the change in modulation, the
right gesture.

Once you perfect your "signature" talk, you'll find you
give every other talk better.

I found this out in two of my most popular talks: "Con-
fessions of a White House Ghost" and "An Evening with
Churchill."

That brings me to a final tip: Give your signature speech
a sexy title, something that titillates interest.

Wimps Pick Limp Titles

Any title that has in it the soggy word "survey" sounds
dreary. "A Survey of Health Planning." Other turnoff titles use words like "perspective," "analysis," or "history."
They're words of the bureaucrats, and that's boring. They
sound academic and "a term-paper title" signals terminal
death in audience interest.

No Bugles, No Trumpets

Years ago a would-be writer approached Somerset Maugham. "Mr. Maugham, you've had great titles for your novels, *Cakes and Ale, Razor's Edge, Moon and Sixpence.* Will you read my manuscript and suggest a title?"

Maugham replied, "Do you have a bugle in your book?"

"No," the puzzled young man answered. "I don't, but I don't see—well, can't you just read my work and—"

"Any trumpets in your piece?" shot back Maugham.

"No, but can't you—"

Maugham interrupted. "Then make your title *No Trumpets, No Bugles.*

Don't make your title "Perspectives on the Life Insurance Industry." Emblazon it. "You Could Live to Ninety."

If you're speaking on buying a house, call your talk "Don't Let Your Dream House Become a Nightmare."

In 1987 I gave speeches across the country honoring the bicentennial of the Constitutional Convention. My title was "What's Happening at the Convention, Dr. Franklin?" A talk I used to deliver to medical groups about authors who also once practiced as physicians I entitled "My Son, the Doctor, I Mean, the Author."

Leadership begins with the label of your talk. Your title as well as your talk should speak the language of leadership.

I n d e x

...

A

abstractions, picture words vs., 62, 65–72
achievement, anecdotes about, 78
action, motivating for, 84
actors, fear experienced by, 16
adages:
  in anecdotes, 141–142
  of Benjamin Franklin, 89
  in Bible, 46–47, 89
advertising, emotional appeal in, 77
Aesop's fables, 71
alibis, as hazard, 18

alliteration, quotations and, 91, 97–98
amenities:
  as opening inanity, 33–34
  time and form of, 34, 35
American Academy of Political Scientists, 12–13
amplifying, in short talks, 83–84
analogies:
  examples of, 64, 65, 66, 69, 70, 72, 92
  exercises in creation of, 65–68
  "incidental recorded accounts" (IRAs) as, 65–66
  Iron Curtain as, 61–63

analogies (*cont.*)
  as mental pictures, 61–72
  PICTURES method and, 67–69
Anderson, Sparky, 140
anecdotes, 63–64
  adages in, 141–142
  animal analogies as, 71
  gossip and, 141
  inspirational, 78
  in introduction, 119–120
  jokes turned into, 136, 137–140,
    143–146
  as opening of speech, 38–39, 49
  self-invented, 143, 145
  three R's rule and, 146
Anglo-Saxon forms of words, 53, 59
animals:
  in metaphors, 98
  in picture analogies, 70–72, 92
antidotes for fear, 17–21
antonyms, *see* contrast, quotations and
Aristotle:
  on analogies, 65
  on humor, 37
  one-theme rule of, 48
  on repetition, 90
Astor, Lady Nancy, 70
athletes, speeches to, 75
audience:
  attention peak of, 33–34
  embarrassed by jokes, 37
  eye contact with, 18, 160
  fears before, 16
  informing of, 21
  mechanism of listening and, 28–29
  speaker's conviction and, 24
  viewed as naked, 17
authority, jokes and, 36

B

Barrymore, Ethel, Churchill advised
    by, 18
Bartlett's Familiar Quotations, 88

Beatitudes, contrast in, 89
beginning, *see* opening of speech
Benchley, Peter, 147
body language, 17–18, 128, 174
"bottom line" of speech:
  distractions from, 47–48
  repeated in closing, 49
  as statement of message, 46, 49
Braddock, Bessie, 138
British Foreign Office motto, 18
Brock, William, 40
Brokaw, Tom, 53, 147, 148
Bryan, William Jennings, 171
  "Cross of Gold" speech of, 172–
    173
bureaucratic jargon, 59
Burton, Richard, 174
Bush, George, 12, 75

C

captions, on slides, 133
caring, 23–25
  as leadership criterion, 151, 155
  mere knowledge vs., 25
  preparedness and, 23–24
Carter, Jimmy, CREAM techniques
    used by, 90–91
case histories, 63–64
  exemplifying by, 82–83
  as opening of speech, 38–39, 49
Center for International Scholars, 45
ceremonial talks:
  of CEOs, 149
  emotions and, 150–151
  preparation of, 150, 151–155
  three M's formula for, 152–153
  time tactic for, 153–155
  at White House, 147–149
Churchill, Sir Winston:
  American politician advised by,
    44
  antipacifist picture analogy of,
    66–67

appeaser picture analogy of, 70
Bartlett's and, 87
on caring about subject, 23–24
classics studied by, 48
CREAM techniques used by, 88,
    89, 90, 92
defects of, 15, 19
on distractions, 47
Dunkirk speech of, 53–54
Eden advised by, 51–52
Eisenhower advised by, 53
emotional ending rule of, 73–79
on euphemisms, 59–60
father figure of, 24
fear-defeating strategies of, 17–
    18, 19
"Finest Hour" speech of, 75
House of Commons opening
    speech of, 41
on impromptu remarks, 114
"Iron Curtain" speech of, 61–63,
    163, 165
Lady Astor and, 70
language of leadership used by,
    13, 32, 41
Macmillan advised by, 45
naked audience tactic of, 17
Nazi metaphor of, 92
1941 speech to Congress by, 40
one-theme rule of, 43–49, 79
Oxford English Dictionary and, 59
pauses as used by, 161
on pedantic language, 52
personal experiences used by, 79
picture words rule of, 61–72, 79
poetic style of, 165
poetry quoted by, 78, 79
private enterprise picture analogy
    of, 71–72
quotations used by, 78, 79, 88
reading of speeches by, 159
setup quotables of, 99
simple language rule of, 51–60, 79
on socialist jargon, 56–57

as source of anecdotes, 137–138
speeches studied by, 31–32
strong beginning rule of, 33–41,
    79
summit picture analogy of, 69
vision of future in speech of, 76
Churchill Memorial (Fulton, Mo.),
    165
Clifford, Clark, 169
Clough, Arthur, 78
Cochran, Bourke, 24
communication:
    as language of leadership, 14
    as oral projection, 29
    by seeing vs. listening, 27–29
    skills vs., 13
concepts, converted to picture analo-
    gies, 62, 65–72
conferences, speaking at, 111–116
Confucius, 114
contractions, 56
contrast, quotations and, 89, 93–94
conversational language and delivery,
    52–53, 56, 160
    eye position and, 161, 162
    pauses in, 161–164
    snapshot/snatch plan for, 160–
        164, 166
    Reagan's use of, 158
    videotaping and, 164
Conwell, Russell, 172, 173
CREAM techniques, 88–98
    alliteration in, 91, 97–98
    contrast in, 89, 93–94
    echo (repetition), in, 90–91, 95–
        97
    metaphor in, 91–92, 98
    rhyme in, 89–90, 94–95
Cuomo, Mario, 16

D

Dale Carnegie School, single-theme
    instruction of, 48

dashes and dots, in speeches vs. articles, 52
Dazzling Dozen, 95–97
"Dear Abby" advice, 40
defiance, fund-raising and, 124
defining problem, 113–116
design (presentation), fund-raising and, 125–126
details, focus vs., 29
dictionary, rhyming, 94
Dirksen, Everett, 161
Disraeli, Benjamin, 31, 43
donations, amount specified in, 126
Dukakis, Michael, 75

E

ear vs. eye, efficiency of, 27–29
EASE strategy, 81–85
    sample outline of, 85
Ecclesiastes, 46–47
echo (repetition), quotations and, 90–91, 95–97
Eden, Anthony, 51–52
Edison, Thomas A., 108
editorials, as opening quotation, 39
Eisenhower, Dwight D., 108, 142
    on "bottom line," 46
    Churchill's advice to, 53
    on MacArthur, 58
electrifying, in short talks, 84–85
eloquence:
    Churchill's emotional ending rule and, 73–79
    sincerity and, 24
emotions:
    athletes motivated by, 75
    in business advertising, 77
    in ceremonial addresses, 150–151
    as "electrifying," 84–85
    fund-raising and, 126
    in heroic acts, 78
    hopeful visions as, 76

in personal experience references, 75–76, 79
    in poetic quotations, 78, 79
    pride as, 74–75, 76
    in speech endings, 73–79, 85
ending of speech:
    "bottom-line" message in, 49
    on emotional note, 73–79, 85
    setting up of, 100–101
energy, fear as, 17
entertainment factor, in speeches, 135–136, 140
euphemisms, 59–60
excuses, as self-defeating, 18
exemplifying, in short talks, 82–83
experience, personal:
    in creating picture analogies, 66
    emotions in, 75–76, 79
    projection of, 29
expertise:
    development of, 176–177
    of speaker, 21, 175
eye contact, 18, 160

F

fear, 15–21
    as energy, 16–17
    expertise vs., 21
    mannerisms and, 17–18
    subject and scope of speech and, 19–21
flattery, praise vs., 34
focusing, of subject matter, 19–21, 29
foolish, looking, 17
Ford, Gerald, memoirs of, 46–47
format of written speeches, 164–166
Four D's for Donors, 124–127
"4-H Club" quotation strategy, 104–110

fragmentizing, report structure and,
113
Franklin, Benjamin, 90, 138–139
adages of, 89
Frost, Robert, 78
fund-raising, 123–128
Four D's for Donors strategy in,
124–127
psychology of, 124, 127, 128
reminders in, 127–128
specifying amounts in, 126
timing in, 126–127

G

Gabor, Zsa Zsa, 139
generalizing, report structure and,
112, 113
gestures:
as "silent" language of leadership,
174
telltale, 17–18
"governmentese," 54
graphs, on slides, 133

H

Hayes, Helen, 16
heart, language of, 78
heroes, quotations and, 104–105
heroics, business, 78
history, quotations and, 106–108
holidays:
quotations and, 108–109
speechmaking opportunities in,
175–176
home, quotations about, 105–106
hope, expression of, 76, 85
horoscope reports, as opening quotation, 40
humor:
Aristotle on, 37
sense of, 36
see also jokes; wit and humor

I

Iacocca, Lee, 13, 49, 107, 172, 173
ideas, projection of, 29
illustrations, on slides, 133
imagery, see picture words
inspiration, in preparation, 152–153
inspirational anecdotes, 78, 83
instant speech formula, 82–85
introductions, 117–121
formula for, 118–120
as portrait, 118, 121
as prologue, 117–118
IRAs (incidental recorded accounts),
65–66
"I" references, 58
"-ize" forms, 53

J

Jackson, Jesse, 89
jargon, 51–60
Jesus Christ, parables of, 64
Johnson, Lyndon B., 147
jokes:
as anecdotes, 136, 137–140,
143–146
audience and speaker embarrassed
by, 37
authority diminished by, 36
three R's and, 146
timing of, 37, 137
when to avoid, 35, 36–37, 136,
137
wit and humor vs., 136

K

Kennedy, John F., 36, 58, 88, 105,
150, 159
CREAM techniques used by, 88,
89, 90, 91
poetry in speeches of, 78
setup quotables of, 99

Kennedy, Robert, brother's eulogy by, 150
Khachigian, Ken, 149
King, Martin Luther, Jr., 36, 55, 88, 161, 172
  CREAM techniques used by, 88, 91
  "I Have a Dream" speech of, 76, 172, 173

L

language of leadership:
  art of communication as, 14
  body language as, 128, 174
  Churchill and, 13, 32, 41
  language of heart as, 78
  in single speech, 172 .
language of speeches:
  Anglo-Saxon vs. Latinate, 53, 59
  Churchill's rule for, 51–60, 79
  contractions in, 56
  as conversational, 52–53, 56
  jargon and, 53, 54, 57, 59
  one-syllable words in, 56, 58, 79, 94
  passive voice in, 53–54
  personal pronouns in, 57–58
  as pictures, 61–72
  as simple, 51–60
  third-person references and, 57–58
  "turtle" words in, 55
Latinate forms of words, 53, 59
leadership:
  achievement of, 12
  active observation and, 107
  caring and, 151, 155
  ceremonial addresses and, 149–150
  emotional language and, 78
  format and, 164–166
  impact of single speech and, 171–172

insights and, 112
management vs., 14
as poise and presence, 128
projection of, 13
secrets of, 107
slide presentations and, 130, 131, 133–134
title of speech and, 178
volunteer speaking services and, 176–177
lecterns, gripping of, 18
Lincoln, Abraham, 31, 69, 99, 148, 153, 159
  CREAM techniques used by, 89, 90
  Gettysburg Address of, 148, 153, 167–168
listening, as inefficient medium, 27–29
Longfellow, Henry Wadsworth, 79

M

MacArthur, Douglas, 36, 58, 159, 161
  West Point speech of, 77
Macmillan, Harold, 45
mannerisms, masking of, 17–18
material in speeches, see subject of speech
Maugham, Somerset, 178
meetings, committee/board, 111–116
  defining problem in, 114–116
  preparation for, 114–116
  recommendations in, 115
  reports for, 111–113
  timing in, 115
Megatrends 1990 (Naisbitt), 49
memorizing speeches, 152, 167–168
memory, 152
  code exercise for, 67–69
  functioning of, 28
message, in preparation, 152

INDEX

metaphors, quotations and, 91–92, 98
middle of speech:
  amenities in, 34, 35
  jokes in, 37, 137
military jargon, 59
mini examples, in amplifying subject, 83
mission, in preparation, 152–153
Mitchell, John, 115
Mondale, Walter, 75
Moore, Edward, 150–151
musical form, as analogy for speeches, 45

N

Naisbitt, John, 49
nakedness, imagination and, 17
nature, in picture analogies, 69
Nehru, Jawaharlal, 104
nerves, nervous energy and, 17
New Testament, 64, 89
Nixon, Richard M., 12
  CREAM techniques used by, 90
  détente picture analogy of, 69
  leaders quoted by, 104
  man in the arena format of, 167
  "Silent Majority" speech of, 164–165
Noonan, Peggy, 149, 159
nostalgia, preparation and, 154–155
notes for speech:
  advantages of, 166–167
  "bottom line" written first in, 46, 49
  format of, 164–166
  memorizing speeches and, 167–168
  organization of ideas in, 168–169
  reading from, 159, 160–164

O

one-syllable words, 56, 58, 79, 94
one theme, Churchill's rule of, 43–49, 79
opening of speech:
  amenities avoided in, 33–34, 35
  case history at, 38–39
  Churchill's rule for, 33–41, 79
  emotional appeal in, 79
  jokes avoided in, 35, 36–37, 136, 137
  powerful statement as, 35
  pregnant pause at, 37–38
  as prime time moment, 37
  quotation at, 38, 39–41
  suspense created at, 39
oral projection, reading aloud vs., 29, 32
orators, successful, 24
Oxford English Dictionary, 59

P

pace, "turtle" words and, 55
page sliding, page turning vs., 166
parables, of Jesus Christ, 64–65
passive voice, avoidance of, 53–54
Paterno, Joe, 75
Paul, Saint, 64
pauses:
  in conversational delivery, 160–164
  exercises using, 163
  pregnant, 37–38
pedantic language, 52
Pennsylvania, University of, 48–49, 159–160, 166–167, 168, 174–175
People magazine, 141
Pepys, Samuel, 55
personality, projection of, 29
personal pronouns, 57–58, 85
persuasive words, 58

pettifogger terms, 56
PICTURES code, in stimulating
    memory, 67–69
picture words, 84, 125, 154
    abstractions vs., 62, 64, 79
    in analogies, 61–72
    from animal characters, 70–72
    Churchill's rule for, 61–72, 79
    entertainers' use of, 68
    in exemplifying message, 83
    exercises in creation of, 65–68
    in fund-raising, 125
    from nature, 69
    in parables, 64–65
    see also analogies
Pitt, William, 31
Podium Humor (Humes), 37
poetry:
    quotations from, 78, 79
    written format of speeches and,
        164–166
pointers, in slide presentations, 133
poise, as language of leadership, 128
politicians:
    analogies used by, 61–72
    emotions used by, 75–76, 77,
        78, 79
    fear experienced by, 16
    poetry used by, 78, 79
pontifical terms, 55–56
Poor Richard's Almanack (Franklin),
    89
praise:
    flattery vs., 34
    parenthetical, 34–35
preparation:
    business meetings and, 113–116
    of ceremonial talks, 150, 151–
        155
    commitment to subject and, 23–
        24, 151–155
    in conversationalizing speech,
        160–165, 166, 169
    memorizing in, 167–168

notes in, see notes for speech
    organization of ideas in, 168–169
    repetition of speech as, 173–174,
        177
    three M's workout in, 152–153
    time tactic in, 153–155
    videotaping and, 164
    volunteering and, 176–177
presence, as language of leadership,
    128
presentation (design), fund-raising
    and, 125–128
pride, expression of, 74–75, 76, 85
prime time moment, 37
problem:
    defining of, 113–116
    solution of, 84
Proverbs, Old Testament, 89
Putnam, Israel, 115–116
"putting on an act," 18

Q

Q & A, material for, 44, 48
QED, 46–47
quotations, 87–101
    choice of, 38, 49
    collecting of, 87–88
    CREAM techniques and, 88–98
    "4-H Club" strategy and, 104–
        110
    humorous impact of, 40
    leaders as source of, 104–107,
        110
    length of, 38
    at opening of speech, 38–41
    from poetry, 78, 79
    self-invented (do-it-yourself), 40–
        41, 92–98
    setting up, 98–100, 101
    shock impact of, 40, 41
    sources for, 39–40, 78, 79, 104–
        110
    theme reinforced by, 49

R

rapid speaking, fear and, 18
Reader's Digest, 16
reading of speeches, 35
   format of written text and, 164–
      166
   by great speakers, 159
   oral projection vs., 29, 32
   page sliding in, 166
   snapshot/snatch plan in, 160–
      164, 166
Reagan, Ronald, 12–13, 171
   ceremonial addresses of, 148–
      149
   emotion in speeches of, 75, 76
   as "Great Communicator," 13, 98
   inspirational endings of, 78
   radio career of, 157–159
   Roosevelt as model of, 158
   setting up lines and, 98–100
   snapshot/snatch plan and, 160
   "Time for Choosing" speech of,
      172
redundancy, *see* repetition
Regan, Donald, economic status
   analogy and, 70
repetition:
   of basic speech, 173–174, 177
   Dazzling Dozen formula for, 95–
      97
   quotations and, 90–91, 95–97
   value of, 29, 49
reports, at business meetings, 111–
   116
   presentation of, 111–112
   technique for, 113
   theme of, 112–113
respect, jokes and, 36
Rhetoric (Aristotle), 48, 65, 90
rhyme, quotations and, 89–90, 94–
   95
rhyming dictionary, 94
Roget's Thesaurus, 98

Roosevelt, Franklin D., 13, 24, 36,
   79, 88, 158, 159, 161
   on Churchill's fighting words, 54
   CREAM techniques used by, 88,
      90, 91, 92
   language of leadership spoken by,
      52
   lend-lease picture analogy of, 69
   setup quotables of, 99
   "Rose Garden Rubbish," 147–149

S

seeing, efficiency of, 27–29
setting up quotable lines, 98–100,
   101
shock effect, in opening quotations,
   40–41
short talks, EASE strategy for, 81–
   85
"signature" speech, 177
simple language, Churchill's rule of,
   51–60, 79
Simpson, O. J., 39–40
sincerity:
   as basis of success, 24
   of praise, 34
slides, 129–134
   dependence on, 131
   do's and don'ts for, 129–130, 133
   leadership role and, 130, 131,
      133–134
   lure of equipment and, 131
   as reinforcing aid, 132
SLIDES (do's and don'ts formula),
   133
slogans, in slide presentations, 133
snapshot/snatch plan, 160–164
   exercises for, 163, 166
solution of problem, in short talks,
   84
Sorensen, Theodore, 94, 159
specifying, in short talks, 84
speech-a-matic strategy, 81–85

speeches, effective:
    Churchill's emotional ending rule
        for, 73–79
    Churchill's one-theme rule for,
        43–49, 79
    Churchill's picture words rule for,
        61–72, 79
    Churchill's simple language rule
        for, 51–60, 79
    Churchill's strong beginning rule
        for, 33–41, 79
    increased by repetition, 172–173
    instant formula for, 81–85
    quotations and, 87–101
speeches, ineffective:
    by Churchill, 19
    detail clutter in, 29
    indications of, 12
    reading articles aloud as, 29, 32,
        35
    weak beginnings in, 33–34
sports stories, at beginning of
    speech, 39–40
staring, fear revealed by, 18
stories in newspaper, at beginning of
    speech, 39
strong beginning, Churchill's rule
    of, 33–41, 79
subject of speech:
    amplifying of, 83–84
    Churchill's five rules and, 33–79
    commitment to, 23–25, 151, 155
    defining of problem and, 113–
        116
    electrifying of, 84–85
    exemplifying of, 82–83
    expertise on, 19, 175, 176
    focusing of, 19–21, 29
    limiting of, 19–20
    preparation of, see preparation
    specifying of, 84
    theme of, see theme
    in written vs. spoken form, 29,
        32, 52

suspense, 78
    at opening of speech, 39
synonyms, books of, 98

T

Thatcher, Margaret:
    "God" and "Queen" in speech for,
        77
    1984 speech to Congress by, 40
theme:
    as "bottom line," 46
    brevity in statement of, 46
    in business reports, 111–112
    Churchill's rule of, 43–49, 79
    Q & A as supplement for, 48
    repetition of, 49
    single, 44, 47, 48, 49
    structuring tips for, 49
third-person usage, 57–58
Thompson, John, 75
three M's formula, in preparation,
    152–153
three R's rule for anecdotes, 146
time tactic, in preparation, 153–155
Time to Heal (Ford), 47
title of speech, do's and don'ts for,
    177–178
Tomlin, Lily, 105
trivia, in preparation, 154–155
Truman, Harry, 107
    speech strategy evolved by, 169–
        170
"turtle" words, 55
Twain, Mark, 58

U

umbrella word/phrase, 49

V

videotaping, use of, 164
vision, hope and, 76

INDEX

visual aids:
  newspaper as, 40
  slides as, 129–134
visualization, *see* picture words
volunteering, advantages of, 176–177
von Bulow, Claus, 28

W

"we" and "you" usage, 85
  third-person reference vs., 57–58
Webster, Daniel, 77
Weizmann, Chaim, 107
White House speech writers, 45–46, 87, 88, 149, 159
  "Rose Garden Rubbish" and, 147–149

"translator" role of, 53
Williams, Ted, 106
wit and humor, 135–146
  in anecdotal form, 136, 137–140, 143–146
  enlightenment feature of, 141
  jokes vs., 136
Wren, Christopher, 109
written forms, speeches vs., 29, 32, 52

Y

yuppy talk, 57

Z

zinger lines, 79
  use of, 100–101

A NOTE ABOUT THE AUTHOR

JAMES HUMES is a communications consultant who travels the country presenting speech seminars to CEOs of major corporations and to government agencies. He had lectured on communication in all of our fifty states and twenty-six foreign countries. He has written speeches for every president from Eisenhower to Bush and is a communications lecturer at the University of Pennsylvania. Humes earned his law degree from George Washington University and has served in the Pennsylvania General Assembly. He has written many books on public speaking as well as a prize-winning biography of Churchill. In 1982 he was a Woodrow Wilson Fellow at the Center for International Scholars at the Smithsonian. When not on tour, he divides his time between his home in Philadelphia and a Washington, D.C., law office.